The Science
of Life

Projects and Principles
for Beginning Biologists

Frank G. Bottone, Jr.

CHICAGO
REVIEW
PRESS

Library of Congress Cataloging-in-Publication Data

Bottone, Frank G.
   The science of life : projects and principles for beginning biologists /
Frank G. Bottone, Jr.
      p. cm.
   Includes bibliographical references and index.
   ISBN 1-55652-382-3
   1. Biology—Experiments—Juvenile literature. [1. Biology—
Experiments. 2. Experiments.] I. Title.
   QH316.5 .B68 2001
   570'.78—dc21

                                                    00-065873

Cover design: Joan Sommers Design
Interior design: Monica Baziuk
Interior illustrations: E. Kulak

Published by Chicago Review Press, Incorporated
814 North Franklin Street
Chicago, Illinois 60610
1-55652-382-3
Printed in the United States of America
5 4 3 2 1

To my favorite aunt, Lisa Behan

Contents

Acknowledgments

MY DEEPEST GRATITUDE goes out to everyone who had an influence on the final outcome of this book. I especially want to thank Stacy Kimberley, Monica Bottone, Jane Katergis, Mair Downing, Kathleen Veness-Meehan, M.D., and of course my parents for all of their kind words, encouragement, and insightful criticisms.

A special thanks goes out to Dr. Paul M. Resslar, professor of biology, Virginia Wesleyan College, for his critical reviews of the manuscript and the inspiration he and Dr. James F. Harris continue to provide to so many students, such as myself, who spent time in the laboratories of Virginia Wesleyan College.

Safety First

THE FIRST LESSON that every beginning biologist should learn is that safety must always come first. Whether you are planning to perform the exercises in this book at home or at school, the first step you should take is to become aware of your surroundings. Begin by making sure there is an adult nearby at all times in the event of an emergency or just to assist you with a procedure. Next, locate a sink with running water in case you get something in your eyes or on your skin and need to rinse the affected area. Finally, look for tripping hazards, such as clutter on the floor of your primary walkways, and remove them. If you are working with a stove or burner, make sure that you have access to water or a fire extinguisher in case of fire.

Here are a few more safety tips.

▶ Never eat or drink anything while you are working on an experiment. Never eat the Jell-O or SlimFast used in this book. The bacteria that you grow on these foods could make you sick.

▶ Never eat fruit from the wild.

▶ Always throw away items such as disposable cups, leaves, sugar solutions, soil, seeds, or any food items as soon as you are finished with them so that you or someone else do not accidentally use or eat these items.

► Iodine is used in this book, and it can be poisonous if you swallow it. If you get any iodine on you, rinse the affected area immediately with water for several minutes and tell an adult. Dispose of any food that has been contaminated with iodine. Dispose of the items once they have been exposed to iodine.

► Always use caution when handling chemicals. Even common household chemicals such as those in Lysol and other disinfectants or antiseptics can be harmful because they may irritate your skin. If you get any on your hands or in your eyes, rinse the affected area immediately with plenty of water.

► Take special precautions when working with plants, insects, and spiders that are naturally found outdoors because they may be poisonous, bite, or cause you to have an allergic reaction. Never experiment with plants such as ivy or mushrooms from the wild—they may be poisonous or cause your skin to break out in a rash. Some spiders, generally those with bright yellow or red markings, are poisonous, so be careful when handling them.

► Only operate a stove or blender under adult supervision and always wear a pair of oven mitts when handling hot liquids.

► Wash your hands before and after each experiment if you take a food break during an experiment.

► If you live in an area where Lyme disease is present, do not perform any outdoor experiments without first getting your parent's permission.

► If you are allergic to mold, do not perform any of the experiments in the chapter about fungi.

Introduction

What Is Biology?

Biology is a fascinating science that helps us understand most of
what we see, hear, feel, and even taste in our world today. All human
beings experience the science of biology firsthand in their everyday
lives although they may not always be aware of it.

In order to become more aware of the biology that surrounds
you, you need to be able to define and understand what biology is.
So you may be asking yourself, what exactly is biology? *Biology* is
the science of life and all that deals with the life of animals and
plants, including their *morphology* (form and structure), *physiology*
(function and activities of their cells and organs), *origin* and *development* (how they grow and reproduce), and *distribution* (where they
live). As you will soon learn, biology encompasses a much wider
range of organisms than just plants and animals. Biology is more
than the study of living organisms. It deals with the compounds
they produce and the reactions they perform. More simply put,

biology is the science of life and the process of studying all that is, or once was, living.

So how do you know if something is living, especially if it is not an animal or if it is a newly discovered organism? In this book, many of the experiments require that you work with living things such as bacteria, worms, insects, and even spiders. You will see that while almost no single definition can describe what it is to be living, "life" is something that you as a biologist can measure and observe. However, something that is living can loosely be defined as something that reacts to changes in its environment, is capable of *respiring* (a complicated word for breathing, which includes forms of breathing not limited to the use of oxygen), and is *organic* (derived from or related to something living).

Biology sometimes has a different meaning to us in our everyday lives. Biology can also be thought of as the interaction of oneself, through all of one's senses, with any of the living or once-living things in our world, in an attempt to gain insight into how they work. Biology is both learning and experiencing the world in which we live. Biology, and its specimens, takes on many forms; some are obvious, some not. For example, the piece of paper that this text is written on has its own biology. It is made from wood pulp that came from a living tree. Each page, therefore, has a history as a living organism. This page has a future biology as well. One day, perhaps a hundred years from now, this book may lie dormant in a landfill with other books that have grown very old. In this landfill, *microorganisms* (tiny animals that cannot be seen with the unaided eye) will begin to degrade the paper, thereby obtaining nutrients so that they can divide and multiply into even more microorganisms. This page will be transformed into part of a new, living organism.

Biology encompasses many more organisms than just animals and plants. In fact, there are five kingdoms of life, and this book is structured so that it includes information about organisms from each of these kingdoms. A *kingdom* is the highest level of classification in biology. Organisms representative of the five kingdoms include the bacteria (Prokaryotae), plants (Plantae), animals (Animalia), fungi (Fungi), and protozoans (Protoctista). Scientists who study these kingdoms are called microbiologists, botanists, zoologists, mycologists, and protozoologists, respectively. If you are interested in a career in one of these branches of science, or you just want to become more aware of the diversity of life that surrounds you, this book will introduce you to the world of biology.

Understanding the Scientific Method

A second theme that you will find throughout this book is that the experiments follow the scientific method, which is used in most every branch of science. The *scientific method* is a series of steps that scientists use to pose questions, design experiments, and form a theory, or "hypothesis," about how the natural world works. It allows future scientists to add validity to the conclusions or disprove them.

As you are performing each experiment in this book, pay close attention to the scientific method, which is organized as follows. First, each experiment has a clearly defined objective, such as what is being measured or observed. Next, the scientist usually lists the materials used in the experiment so that others can repeat it and so they do not forget how they performed the experiment. A detailed procedure is always included because most scientific experiments are too complex to perform without some notes on the best way to repeat it. Finally, the results are recorded. In this book you will find some expected results. However, sometimes something totally bizarre happens that is more interesting than the expected result. Therefore, it is important to keep track of your results in a notebook to compare them with other experiments and to help you understand the scientific method and themes throughout this book.

One of the most important procedures in the scientific method is the use of controls during an experiment. A *control sample* is a sample that does not undergo any treatment. In a *controlled experiment* you limit the variables among treatment groups. For example, if you want to know if sunlight affects plant growth, you would use two almost identical plants of the same variety and place one in the sun and one in the shade and measure them both in the same way. An even better experiment would be to place several plants in varying degrees of sunlight for a specified period of time each day. And you may also want to make sure no animals or pests interfere with the plants if they are outdoors. So, you see, there are many ways to control an experiment, and the more controls the better. However, it is not always feasible to use more than one control such as in many of the experiments in this book. More controls make experiments more complicated and expensive.

Before you begin the first experiment, you need to know how to gather and document data in a scientific way so that you and others will be able to trust the results of your experiment. As a scientist, I want to see for myself how a fellow scientist performed an experiment before I feel confident in the results.

Before you learn how to gather and collect data, you should understand and appreciate the importance of a laboratory notebook. Your laboratory notebook will allow you to make difficult calculations and describe how you performed the experiment, which will be useful later. This is especially important when something does not work or if you wish to repeat a successful experiment. Always write down as much information as you can about each experiment, including the date and time, the materials used, and the expected and actual results.

The first experiment in this book is intended to illustrate this process. One of the best ways to organize the scientific information is to make a data table. You will collect data in this way when you perform the experiments in this book. A *data table* is a ledger that is organized in columns and rows for you to write down data, or information, that you collect and things you observe, such as when you begin and finish the experiment, how much starting material was used, and the results you found. To do so, you will need a laboratory notebook to gather information and make calculations during each experiment throughout this book. Any notebook will work fine.

As a scientist, you are responsible for documenting the results of each experiment, analyzing them, and keeping track of how each experiment was performed. The information you collect should be clear, concise, and easy to understand so that others can understand the experiment in the future, especially if you get some unusual results, which is often the case.

Below is an example of a data table similar to the kind that you may want to use when performing the experiments throughout this book. The kind of data shown in the sample data table is similar to the data you will collect in the first experiment of this book, which follows this introduction. You can make a data table in your laboratory notebook using a marker and a ruler. As an alternative, you can use graph paper.

In the back of this book you will find a table of conversions, including information on converting gallons to liters, inches to centimeters, and quarts to ounces (page 109). Remember to refer to it at any time during the course of your experiments. Here's a sample data table:

SAMPLE NAME	TIME IN	TIME OUT	WEIGHT	IRON COLLECTED
Control	9:00	9:20	None	None
Fish	9:30	9:40	490g	Lost some sample, but still not as much iron as liver
Liver	9:10	9:20	500g	A lot of iron

Iron in Your Food

Iron, nickel, and cobalt are magnetic elements commonly found in soil. Unlike cobalt and nickel, iron is a micronutrient required by most plants, animals, and other organisms. Plants can absorb iron from the soil. However, animals have to obtain iron as well as other trace nutrients from their diet. In animals, iron is primarily found in cytochromes, which are proteins found in the energy-producing mitochondria (parts within the cells) of animal cells, and hemoglobin, a pigment that gives blood its characteristic red color. Iron is a component of several plant proteins, such as cytochromes, and ferredoxin, which are pigments used during respiration. Although iron is not a component of chlorophyll, it plays a vital role in its *synthesis* (the production of a substance).

Objective

Learn how to properly set up a biology science experiment designed to compare the amount of iron that can be extracted from two different food items.

Materials

- Measuring cup
- 2 cups (500 grams) fresh beef liver
- Blender
- 9 cups (2.25 liters) water, plus additional water for rinsing tweezers
- String
- 2 round magnets, 1 inch (2.5 centimeters) in diameter with a hole in the center
- Tweezers
- White paper
- Magnifying glass
- 2 cups (500 grams) fresh fish

✳ Adult supervision recommended

Place the liver in a blender containing 3 cups (750 milliliters) of water. Attach a piece of string to one of the magnets by placing it through the hole in the center of the magnet. Tie both ends of the string onto the handle of the blender using a double knot so that the magnet is suspended from the top of the blender and will not fall into the bottom of the blender *(see figure 0.1)*.

Dangle the magnet into the blender so that it just reaches the top of the water. Secure the lid onto the blender so that the magnet will not slip down into the blades.

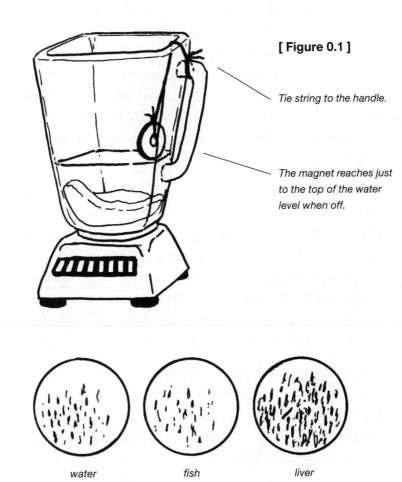

[Figure 0.1]

Tie string to the handle.

The magnet reaches just to the top of the water level when off.

water   fish   liver

Once you are certain that the magnet is safe and secure, carefully turn the blender on low while visually checking that the magnet does not interfere with the blades of the blender. If it does, unplug it at once, shorten the string, and begin again. Blend the solution on low for 15 minutes. Do not leave the blender unattended.

Turn off the blender, grab the string, and then remove the lid. Carefully dip the magnet into a cup of water to rinse off any excess liver. You may want to use a pair of tweezers to pick off the last bits of liver. Place the magnet onto a piece of white paper. Draw a circle 1 inch (2.5 centimeters) in diameter in the upper right hand corner of the paper. Write the word *liver* underneath this circle.

Can you see any of the iron (and some other metals) accumulated on the magnet? Allow the two magnets to stick together and then pull the two magnets apart so that the second magnet is just above the surface of the first. Slide the top magnet back and forth. This will make the flakes of iron stand on end. For this to work, you must hold the magnets together so that the sides that are magnetically attracted to each other are closest. The iron will appear like tiny, brownish-red blades of grass.

Place the magnet on the piece of paper. With a magnifying glass in one hand and a pair of tweezers in the other, try to remove as many of the iron flakes as you can and then place them in the circle for liver you drew on the corner of the paper. If you cannot see the iron, let the magnets dry on a windowsill for 10 minutes and try again. Rinse out the blender and the magnets, and then repeat the experiment first with water alone (as a control) and then again with the same amount of fish and fresh water (for comparison).

Compare the amount of iron you extracted from each item. Liver and fish both contain enough iron so that you should be able to see it easily with a magnifying glass. Try to determine which of equal amounts of fish and liver contains more iron by visually comparing circles on the page.

Results

Which substance, fish or liver, appears to contain more iron in the same amount of tissue? Liver is high in iron because it uses iron to filter red blood cells, which contain hemoglobin bound to iron. Did you notice any iron in the control (water) experiment? If so, do you think water has enough iron in it for you to see or would it be better explained as carryover from the liver?

Variations

What other foods do you think might be high in iron? Determine if cereal is high in iron. Compare different types of cereal to see if they contain different amounts of iron. Try one cereal made from wheat, another made from rice, and a third made from corn. Measure equal amounts of the different kinds of cereal by weight so that you can compare them more accurately. Alternatively, you could measure them by volume by crushing the cereal into a cup using a spoon and repeating the process using the same volume with the other cereals. Compare your results using a magnifying glass.

> ▶ *On average, humans contain about 4.5 grams of iron, mainly in their hemoglobin. Not all animals use iron and hemoglobin to carry their oxygen. Some invertebrates (animals without a spinal column) make a protein called hemocyanin, which contains copper instead of iron as its oxygen-binding compound. These invertebrates have blue blood instead of red. Some annelid worms have green blood due to the presence of a pigment called chlorocruorin, while others contain the pigment hemoglobin, just like humans.*

Bacteria Are Everywhere

(Kingdom Prokaryotae)

Microbiology is the study of microscopic organisms, which are organisms that you cannot see with the unaided eye. Bacteria are the most common form of microscopic organisms. Bacteria are found in soil and water, on the surfaces of plants and animals, and even on you. Bacteria and the related blue-green algae (also known as cyanobacteria) belong to the kingdom Prokaryotae (formerly Monera). The word *Prokaryotae* comes from the Greek word *prokaryon*, which means "before a nucleus." (A *nucleus* is the structure within a cell that contains genetic material and is found in all creatures except those in this kingdom.) Since prokaryotes do not have a nucleus to contain genetic material, the material is located within the cell along with the rest of the cellular material.

Bacteria serve an integral role in nature and everyday life. Bacteria, along with other organisms, *decompose* (break down) dead material such as leaves and other tissues on the forest floor, in rivers and streams, and in your own backyard. For example, have you ever noticed that every autumn, leaves accumulate on the ground, and by the next spring they are almost gone? This is in part due to decomposition by bacteria. Without decomposition, nutrients called vitamins and minerals wouldn't become available when an organism dies. It is through decomposition of dead material, animal waste, and other tissue that nutrients are returned to the soil. These important compounds are then available for other living organisms such as plants.

Bacteria are also significant to our lives because they can cause diseases, produce food and medicine, and are used to research human diseases. Bacteria that cause disease are often referred to as "germs." Germs are what we call bacteria or viruses that make us sick. However, most bacteria do not make us sick. In fact, many bacteria are beneficial to us. Bacteria on the surface of our skin and mouth help to prevent germs from attaching and growing on these surfaces. The beneficial bacteria are able to do this by outnumbering the germs. Luckily, most bacteria do not cause disease. Beneficial bacteria are also used in the production of medicines, such as antibiotics, foods, such as sauerkraut and cottage cheese, and fuels, such as methane gas. *Antibiotics* are chemicals used to kill or inhibit the growth of unwanted microorganisms. Antibiotics are prescribed by doctors and are found in over-the-counter ointments. However, doctors and scientists were not the first ones to use antibiotics. Bacteria, yeast, and especially fungi have been producing antibiotics to kill one another long before we discovered uses for them.

Growing Bacteria

Even though bacteria are microscopic, you can grow them at home the way that scientists grow them in the laboratory in order to study them. Because bacteria can grow quickly and reach very high numbers in a short period of time, they are easy to study. Bacteria *divide* (split from one to two cells) about every 30 minutes. If just one cell were to continue to divide at this rate, there would be 1,048,576 cells in just 10 hours. That's a lot of bacteria. However, many factors such as nutrients, predation, and space limit this outrageous growth.

There are many different ways to grow microorganisms in the laboratory. When scientists grow microorganisms such as bacteria, they refer to the bacteria as a *culture*. The material used to grow the microorganisms is called *culture medium*. Culture medium contains all the essential nutrients needed to support bacterial growth, such as sugar, protein, vitamins, and minerals. A liquid culture is often called a broth, while a solid culture is called an agar dish. *Agar*, the most common form of culture medium, is a gelling agent used to grow bacteria on. Agar often contains agarose, which comes from certain seaweeds.

Objective

Make a culture medium using gelatin from Jell-O instead of agar. Use the culture medium to determine if your arm, a bathroom countertop, or soil contains more bacteria by growing bacteria from each on a solid form of growth medium.

Materials for Bacterial Growth Medium

- ► 1 box Jell-O, any flavor
- ► $1\frac{1}{2}$ cups water
- ► $\frac{1}{2}$ cup SlimFast liquid
- ► Measuring cup
- ► Stove or burner
- ► 3-quart (3-liter) pot
- ► Large bowl
- ► Large spoon
- ► 4 disposable cups
- ► Plastic wrap
- ► 4 rubber bands

Materials for the Experiment

- ► Water, sanitized by boiling and allowed to cool while covered
- ► 4 cotton swabs
- ► 1 cup fresh, moist soil from your backyard
- ► Marker
- ► Lamp

*   *Adult supervision recommended*

Making the Bacterial Growth Medium

Begin the experiment by washing all of the cups and utensils with soap and warm water to remove any microorganisms that may already be present.

Under adult supervision, prepare the Jell-O according to the instructions on the package with the following exception: replace $\frac{1}{2}$ cup cold water with $\frac{1}{2}$ cup liquid SlimFast. The SlimFast will provide the bacteria with the essential vitamins and nutrients normally found in medium but not found in Jell-O.

After adding all of the ingredients, stir mixture once every 2 minutes with a large spoon for at least 15 minutes so that the solution cools, but remains well mixed. Fill each of the disposable cups with $\frac{1}{2}$ cup of the Jell-O mixture. Immediately after pouring the medium into the cups, cover each cup with plastic wrap. Place a rubber band around the plastic wrap to hold it in place.

Refrigerate the cups for at least 3 hours to allow the bacterial growth medium to solidify.

Performing the Experiment

Once the medium has hardened, collect microorganisms to add to the medium as follows.

Moisten a cotton swab by dipping one end into a cup of the boiled water. The reason you want to use water that was previously boiled is to be certain that there are no bacteria growing in it. (Boiling kills most bacteria.) Rub the moistened cotton swab on your arm. Carefully remove the plastic wrap from one of the cups. Quickly rub the same end of the cotton swab in a *Z* pattern across the surface of the medium *(see figure 1.1)*.

Replace the plastic wrap and rubber band to minimize the chance of any other bacteria finding their way onto the medium.

Repeat this process two more times using a new cotton swab and a new cup from a bathroom countertop and from a cup of soil from your backyard. Do not rub any bacteria on the last cup. You will use this one as a control, or for comparison. Label the cups with the original location of the bacteria such as "arm," "countertop," "soil," and "control." Place the cups somewhere slightly warmer than room temperature, such as under a lamp. However, do not place the cups on a stove because the medium might melt. Let the cultures grow for 2 days so that you can see them

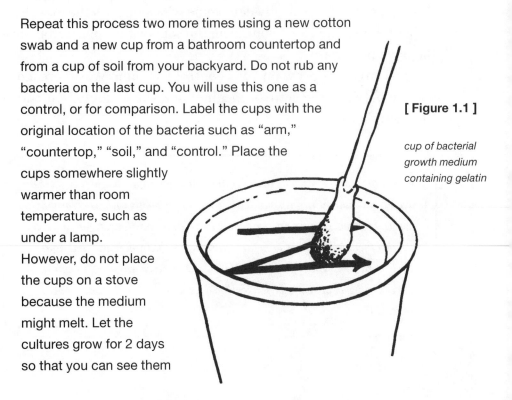

[Figure 1.1]

cup of bacterial growth medium containing gelatin

accumulate. If you do not see anything, wait another 2 days. Bacteria should grow very well on this medium if it is left in a warm place.

Bacteria will look like a slimy trail where you wiped the cotton swab. Although you should find mostly bacteria, sometimes fungi may grow, too. Bacteria usually appear as white or yellow dots on the surface of the medium. Fungi will look like a fuzzy carpet with black or green tips growing out of the medium. These are known as fungal mycelia, which you will learn more about in chapter 4.

Results

What did you find growing on your medium? Can you see bacteria growing in a Z pattern on the surface of the medium? Compare the three cups and then visually determine which one has the most bacteria growing on it. Did your arm, the soil, or the countertop have the most bacteria?

Did anything grow on your control medium? Was there a difference between the control medium and the medium you added the bacteria to?

> ▶ *Agarose (also known as agar) is derived from algae. Algae are fresh-water and marine organisms. They contain pigments such as chlorophyll, which is green, or phycobilins, which are red. Some algae are microscopic while others, such as seaweed, are quite large. Did you know that agar and carrageen, which are derived from red seaweed, are used as thickeners in a variety of foods such as jelly, soup, ice cream, and even the icing on cakes?*

Variations

Can you think of any other places where bacteria might grow? Keep in mind that bacteria thrive in warm and wet places. Compare the amount of bacteria on two different surfaces in your backyard that are of interest to you by growing them on bacterial growth medium, as you did in this experiment. Determine if there are more bacteria growing on dead leaves from the top or the bottom of a pile of leaves. The growth medium that results in the most bacterial growth likely had more bacteria on it. Where else would you expect to find a lot of bacteria?

Hand Washing

Recently, a new group of hand soaps called waterless hand soaps have become available. They are unique because they do not require the use of running water. Therefore, they are a convenient way of killing microorganisms on your skin when a sink is not available. The active ingredient in most waterless hand sanitizers is 60–70 percent alcohol, which evaporates from your skin within a few minutes after use.

Objective

Compare the effectiveness of ordinary hand washing to hand washing with waterless hand soap. Determine how effectively your ordinary hand soap works at preventing bacteria from growing on growth medium after washing your hands.

Materials

- Liquid hand soap
- Waterless hand soap
- Label tape
- Marker
- Lamp
- 3 disposable cups with prepared bacterial growth medium *(see page 4)*

Do not wash your hands for at least 1 hour before you continue with this experiment. This is to ensure that there are plenty of healthy bacteria growing on your skin. Using a piece of label tape, label 3 cups of growth medium as "control" (no soap), "hand soap," and "waterless soap" respectively.

Gently wipe your fingertips on the surface of 1 cup of medium. Quickly replace the plastic wrap and rubber band. Wash your left hand by placing a pea-sized drop of liquid hand soap in your palm and then massage it all over the palm of this hand by using your fingertips from the same hand. Gently rinse your left hand under running tap water. Wait 2–3 minutes for your hand to dry, then wash your right palm with an equal amount of waterless hand soap in the same manner. Do rinse your right hand with running water.

Let your right hand dry for 2–3 minutes as well, although it should dry much faster than the hand washed with water because waterless hand soap contains alcohol, which evaporates from the heat given off by your skin. After washing each hand individually, remove the plastic wrap and rubber band from each cup, then gently wipe your fingertips on the surface of the growth medium inside the appropriately labeled cup. Place the cups under a lamp for 2 days. Determine which soap is better at killing microorganisms by estimating the amount of bacteria growing on them. The one with the least bacteria is the best hand soap.

Results

How well did you wash your hands? Did hand washing reduce the number of bacteria that were able to grow? Which hand soap was more effective at killing bacteria? The cup with the least amount of bacteria growing on it was the most effective.

Antiseptics and Disinfectants

Have you ever scraped your knee while running around in the yard? If so, you may have applied an antiseptic such as hydrogen peroxide, antibacterial hand soaps, or rubbing alcohol to the scrape. This kills the germs, thus preventing them from getting into the wound. *Antiseptics* are chemicals that destroy a wide variety of germs. The root word *septic* comes from the word *sepsis* meaning "infection." Antiseptics are a class of disinfectants that are safe and mild enough to use on your skin. As a result, they are only moderately effective at the removal and killing of microorganisms.

Antiseptics work in a variety of ways. Soap increases the effectiveness of hand washing by helping to dissolve and break up the natural oils that are found on your skin as well as removing and killing bacteria and some viruses. While the physical act of scrubbing is moderately effective at removing bacteria from your hands, without the aid of soap, literally millions of bacteria can survive in the tiny cracks of your hands. The physical act of scrubbing, the effectiveness of the soap, and how long you wash your hands are all very important factors in the removal of microorganisms from your skin. Hydrogen peroxide works by breaking down in the presence of heat from your skin into a form that is deadly to some bacteria.

When hydrogen peroxide breaks down, it is converted into water and a special form of oxygen that bubbles.

Disinfectants are chemicals used to kill or inhibit the growth of microorganisms on objects such as countertops, floors, and sinks. They are too strong to use on your skin. Some common household disinfectants include Lysol, detergents, and bleach. Alcohol (ethanol) is the main ingredient (by weight) in Lysol. It works by disrupting the outer surface of the microorganism and thereby killing it. It also contains a complex compound used as a germicide, to kill germs such as bacteria, viruses, and molds on nonliving surfaces. You can test these products to see which one is more effective at killing or inhibiting the growth of bacteria.

Objective

Determine which household antiseptic is more effective at killing or inhibiting the growth of microorganisms from soil on medium, hydrogen peroxide or Lysol.

Materials

- Label tape
- 2 disposable cups with prepared bacterial growth medium *(see page 4)*
- Marker
- 4 cotton swabs
- Hydrogen peroxide (3 percent solution)
- Water, sanitized by boiling and allowed to cool while covered
- 1 cup fresh, moist soil from your backyard
- Lysol disinfectant spray
- 1 index card
- Lamp

∗   *Adult supervision recommended*

Wrap a piece of label tape around two cups filled with bacterial growth medium. Using the marker, label one cup "hydrogen peroxide" and the other "Lysol."

For the hydrogen peroxide cup, draw a vertical line on the outside of a cup dividing it into two equal halves. Label the left side of a cup "hydrogen peroxide" and the right side "control." Dip one end of the cotton swab into the hydrogen peroxide. Remove the rubber band and plastic wrap from the cup labeled hydrogen peroxide and then gently rub the cotton swab across the medium on the appropriately labeled side of the cup. Add just enough of the hydrogen peroxide so that it does not spread onto the control half of the cup. (Do not get any hydrogen peroxide on the control side of the medium.) Quickly replace the plastic wrap and rubber band.

For the Lysol cup, label the left side of the second cup "Lysol" and the right side "control." Place an index card at the center of the surface of the growth medium and spray the side labeled "Lysol" with Lysol. (Do not get any Lysol on the control side of the medium.) Quickly replace the rubber band and plastic wrap *(see figure 1.2a)*.

[Figure 1.2a]

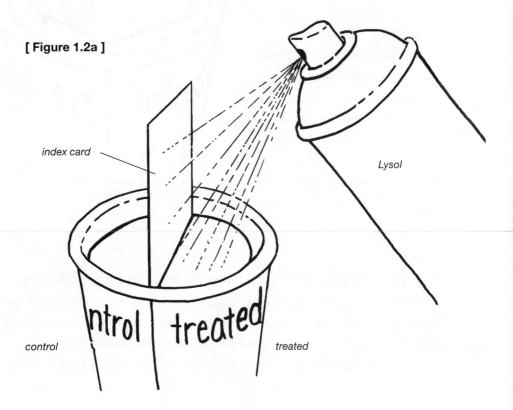

index card

Lysol

control

treated

Moisten two new cotton swabs by dipping one end of each into a cup of the boiled water. Dip the cotton swabs into the soil and stir them around so that the tips are covered in soil. Shake any excess soil off the cotton swabs.

Remove the rubber band and plastic wrap from the cup labeled hydrogen peroxide and gently rub the soil-covered end of the cotton swab in a *V* pattern across the surface of the medium *(see figure 1.2b)*. Start from the control side and move across to the treated side of the cup. This is so that you do not drag any of the antiseptic onto the control side. Do the same with the second cotton swab on the cup labeled "Lysol." Quickly replace the plastic wrap and rubber band so that no bacteria accidentally find their way onto the medium, and then place the cups under a lamp. Wait 2 days and see what grows. If you do not see anything, wait an additional 2 days.

[Figure 1.2b]

Note "V" pattern and direction of stroke.

Results

Was the hydrogen peroxide or Lysol disinfectant more effective at inhibiting the growth of microorganisms? If the bacteria grew on the control side but was unable to grow on the treated side, it was effective. How well did the bacteria grow on the control sides? Was the growth partially or totally inhibited on the treated sides of the cups?

> ▶ *The first disinfectant widely used in a hospital setting was phenol, introduced by Joseph Lister in 1867. Listerine was named after him. As a result of using phenol, Joseph Lister developed aseptic surgery. "Aseptic" means without unwanted life: without microorganisms. Before this discovery, doctors did not know that germs on their hands and instruments caused infections in their patients. Phenol is no longer used because it is toxic, has a strong odor, and is irritating to the skin.*

Variations

Determine how well some other common household antiseptics and disinfectants work. Choose two different types of antiseptics or disinfectants and grow bacteria from your bathroom sink using a moist cotton swab. Determine which one works best by comparing the amount of bacteria that grow on each medium cup. The one with the least growth worked best.

Bacteria and Antibiotics

Antibiotics were first discovered by Alexander Fleming when a fungus contaminated, then killed, several colonies of bacteria on an agar dish. You can grow microorganisms in the presence of various antibiotics to test their resistance or susceptibility to them. An organism is said to be resistant to an antibiotic if it is able to grow in its presence. If the organism cannot grow, it is said to be susceptible. Doctors and scientists have become increasingly concerned about antibiotic resistance among bacteria that cause illnesses. This means that antibiotics will be less effective in fighting illnesses. In order to slow this trend, prescription antibiotics should be taken as instructed by a physician, in the appropriate dose, and only when absolutely necessary. Unlike antiseptics, antibiotics take some time to work because they have to be absorbed by the bacteria. Once absorbed, they act in a variety of ways to interfere with the normal growth of the bacterium.

Objective

Determine if Neosporin or bacitracin is better at preventing the growth of microorganisms.

Materials

- ▶ 4 cotton swabs
- ▶ Water, sanitized by boiling and allowed to cool while covered
- ▶ 4 disposable cups filled with bacterial growth medium
- ▶ Marker
- ▶ Aluminum foil, 12-inch (30-centimeter) square
- ▶ 1-ounce (28-gram) tube of Neosporin
- ▶ 1-ounce (28-gram) tube of bacitracin
- ▶ Label tape
- ▶ 1 manila folder
- ▶ Hole puncher
- ▶ Tweezers
- ▶ Rubbing alcohol (70 percent)
- ▶ Ruler
- ▶ Paper towels
- ▶ Lamp

✳   Adult supervision recommended

Dip one cotton swab in the cup of water. Pick a spot on your arm and rub the swab across the surface of your skin several times. Quickly remove the plastic wrap and rub the same end of the cotton swab over the *entire surface* of the medium. Repeat this process with two more cups.

Place some aluminum foil on a clean, level surface. Squirt a pea-sized drop of the bacitracin and Neosporin next to each other on the corner of a piece of aluminum foil. Label each drop of antibiotic ointment by writing its name on a piece of tape, then placing it next to the drop of ointment. Label the cups "bacitracin," "Neosporin," and "control."

Wash your hands thoroughly. Take out a clean manila folder from its packaging. While holding the manila folder over the aluminum foil, punch nine holes in it so that the paper disks fall onto the aluminum foil. Do not touch the paper disks with your hands because they need to remain as clean as possible.

Sterilize a pair of tweezers by soaking them in a solution of rubbing alcohol in one of the cups for 2 minutes. Remove the tweezers from the alcohol, and then allow them to air dry for 15 seconds. Using the pair of tweezers, pick up one paper clipping at a time and scoop up enough bacitracin to cover the bottom surface of the piece of manila folder *(see figure 1.3)*.

The disks are now called "antibiotic disks." Add an equal amount of bacitracin to each antibiotic disk so that you can compare them later.

Quickly place three antibiotic disks, containing the same antibiotic, onto the

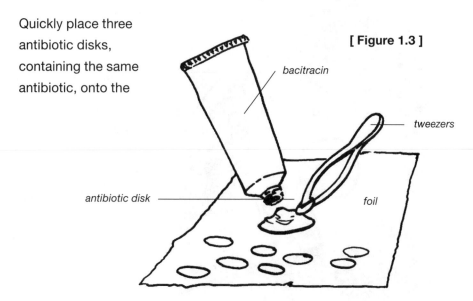

[Figure 1.3]

bacitracin

tweezers

antibiotic disk

foil

surface of the appropriately labeled cup with the side containing the antibiotic facing down as shown *(see figure 1.4)*.

Clean the tweezers with a paper towel before each use. Repeat this with the Neosporin, making sure to resterilize the tweezers each time you use them. Add three disks that do not contain any antibiotics on them to the control cup. Place the cups of medium under a lamp for 2 days and then see what grows.

If the antibiotics are effective, the bacteria should not be able to grow in the area immediately around the

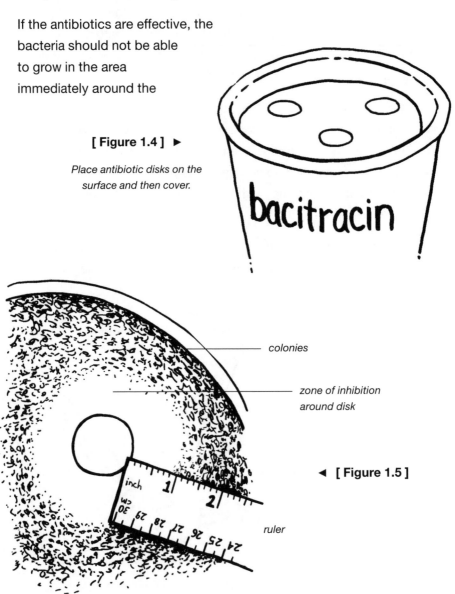

[Figure 1.4] ▶

Place antibiotic disks on the surface and then cover.

bacitracin

colonies

zone of inhibition around disk

◀ **[Figure 1.5]**

ruler

antibiotic disks. This area is called a zone of inhibition and is a result of the antibiotic spreading out from the disk into the medium, inhibiting the bacteria. Measure the diameter of the zone of inhibition using a ruler *(see figure 1.5)*.

Results

Assuming you spread the same amount of bacteria on each of the surfaces, the antibiotic with the largest zone of inhibition is likely the most effective antibiotic on the strains of bacteria you grew. This is because bacteria are present in the zone, but they are not able to grow enough to form colonies that you can see with the unaided eye. Which antibiotic was most effective? How did they compare to the control?

Variations

Some bacteria are resistant to antibiotics. Compare the susceptibility of bacteria from different sources, such a bathroom counter, the keypad of an automated teller machine, to Neosporin, bacitracin, and another household antibiotic. If the bacteria are able to grow in and around the antibiotic, they may be resistant (or there may be too much bacteria or not enough antibiotic). Apply the same

▶ *Antibiotics are chemicals that kill or inhibit the growth of microorganisms such as bacteria, fungi, and protozoans. Until recently, there were no drugs for the treatment of viruses. However, as a result of the onset of AIDS (acquired immunodeficiency syndrome), several new drugs have been discovered and released onto the market that work against viruses. Unfortunately, they are not nearly as effective as antibiotics were when they were first discovered.*

amount of bacteria to each cup so that you can compare them using the diameter of the zones of inhibition. You can also determine if the bacteria can grow in the presence of a triple antibiotic ointment (an antibiotic cream that contains three antibiotics) such as Triple Antibiotic Ointment or other brands sold over the counter at most drugstores.

2

Plants Grow, Move, and Respond to the Environment

(Kingdom Plantae)

We live in a world filled with plants. Plants are not able to walk or talk, but they definitely shape, modify, and interact with the world around us. Plants sense and respond to movement, touch, vibration, and light. They serve an integral role in the recycling of water through a process known as transpiration, and they contain medicines used to heal us when we're sick. Plants are directly or indirectly responsible for producing all of the food we eat. Humans benefit from plants in a variety of other ways. We harvest plants as crops, use their wood for shelter in our homes, and we make paper money out of plant fibers called flax.

Almost every plant undergoes photosynthesis. *Photosynthesis* is the process by which plants convert energy from the sun into chemical (or food) energy such as sugars. During this process, plants consume carbon dioxide. In turn, they add oxygen back to the air. Most plants contain a compound called chlorophyll. Plants with this compound use it to undergo the process of photosynthesis. In this process, chlorophyll absorbs light and converts solar energy into chemical energy in the form of simple sugars. In this way, plants can make sugar that can be converted into many of the nutrients their tissues require. Plants provide a great number of organisms such as animals, fungi, and microorganisms with food. The importance of plants to our environment and all of the living things in it cannot be understated.

Transpiration

Animals and plants can go a long time without food. However, the same is not true with water. In fact, every living thing needs water. If an animal goes several days without drinking water, it will get sick. If you do not water an indoor plant, it will wilt, turn brown, and then die. When animals are thirsty, they search for a water supply and drink from it. But how do plants find and drink water?

Plants use roots, buried within the soil, to locate and collect water. Once the roots reach a water supply, the water travels through the plant roots, stem, branches, and leaves, where it then evaporates. The loss of water vapor from a plant is called transpiration. It is the process that causes water to move through the plant. Because of this process, a plant actually requires more water than an animal of the same weight. This is largely because plants do not recycle their water. Animals such as humans do not need to transpire water because they have a circulatory system (a network through which nutrients and waste travel to all parts of the body). You can watch a flower transpire water containing a dye and measure how much water it transpires. Factors that affect transpiration in plants include humidity, wind, temperature, internal carbon dioxide concentrations, and the structure of each different type of plant.

Objective

Learn about a process known as transpiration and then determine how long it takes an ordinary flower to transpire its own weight in water.

Materials

- Small kitchen scale capable of measuring less than 1 pound (500 grams)
- 2 fresh white carnations
- Notebook
- 2 clear plastic bottles, 1-quart (1-liter) size
- Measuring cup
- Water
- Food coloring
- Marker
- Plastic wrap
- 2 rubber bands
- Calculator (recommended)

Using a kitchen scale, weigh each flower and record its weight in your notebook. Fill two bottles with 17 ounces (500 milliliters) of water using a measuring cup. Add 6 drops of food coloring to the water in one of the bottles. The bottle without any coloring will serve as a control to see how much water evaporates without a flower put in it. Put the stem of a flower into the bottle containing the water and food coloring. Draw a line to mark the level of the water after adding the flower to the bottle. Mark the level of the control bottle also. Wrap a small piece of plastic wrap around each of the openings to the bottles to prevent the water from evaporating *(see figure 2.1)*. Secure the plastic wrap using a rubber band.

Note the time you added the flower to the bottle. Watch as the flower transpires the colored water and determine how many hours it takes the water to reach the top of the flower. You will be able to tell when the water reaches the top of the flower because the dye will change the color of the flower's petals.

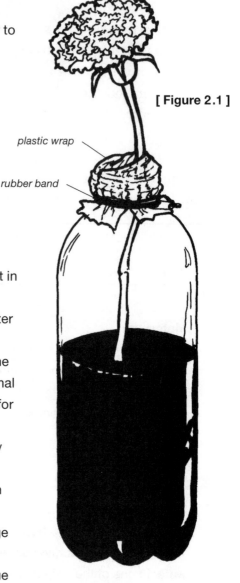

[Figure 2.1]

plastic wrap

rubber band

Determine how many days it takes the plant to transpire its own weight in water as follows. Wait 2 days, then remove the flower and pour the water back into the measuring cup. Write down the new volume of water in the bottle and subtract it from the original volume. Repeat this measurement for the control bottle to see how much was lost due to evaporation directly from the bottle and not through the plant. If you did not see a change in the control bottle, use a zero in the formula below. If there was a change in the control bottle, record the change, and then subtract that value from the change in volume in the flower bottle you previously calculated. This is because that amount of water was not lost due to transpiration but rather evaporation from the top of the bottle and/or losses due to the experimental process itself.

This value is the volume transpired by the flower over the period of time you examined. Pour the water back into the appropriate bottle, put the flower back, and replace the plastic wrap. If you did not see much of a change in the bottle with the flower in it, repeat the measurements again in 2 days.

To calculate how long it takes the flower to transpire its own weight in water, divide the weight of the flower by the volume of water the flower transpired in one day. For the purpose of this experiment, it is safe to assume that 1-ounce liquid measure of water is equal to 1-ounce solid measure of flower. For example, assume the flower transpired 3.3 ounces (100 milliliters) and 0.3 ounce (10 milliliters) evaporated from the total of 17 ounces (500 milliliters) in the bottle over the course of 2 days, then it would take a 7-ounce (200-gram) flower the following amount of days to transpire its own weight in water. The same calculation is offered in metric units.

(17 ounces – 13.6 ounces) – 0.3 ounce	= 3.0 ounces,
3.0 ounces ÷ 2 days	= 1.5 ounces/day,
Therefore, 7 ounces ÷ 1.5	= 4.6 days.

(500 milliliters – 400 milliliters) – 10 milliliters	= 90 milliliters
90 milliliters ÷ 2 days	= 45 milliliters/day
Therefore, 200 grams ÷ 45	= 4.4 days

Using the formula above, determine how many days it would take the flower in your experiment to transpire its own weight in water.

▶ *Plants require a great deal of water because so much is lost through the tiny holes in their leaves called* stomata. *In fact, some trees are capable of transpiring water at 75 centimeters per minute. This has a cooling affect on the surrounding air. The air in a forest can sometimes be 18°–27°F (10°–15°C) cooler than that in the surrounding grasslands.*

Results

How long did it take for your flower to transpire its own weight in water? How much water do you think a large tree such as an oak or pine tree transpires? How long do you think it would take a pine tree to transpire its own weight in water?

Variations

How long do you think it would take you to drink your own weight in water? Remember, drinking is much different than transpiration. You can calculate how long it would take you to drink your own weight in water by recording the volume of everything you drink and adding it up until it reaches your own weight. Assume 1 gallon (4 liters) is equal to 9 pounds (2.2 kilograms) and keep in mind that this is only a rough approximation. Can you think of a better way to account for the water content of food as well?

Germinating Seeds

Do you have any tall trees such as an oak tree in your yard or in a nearby park? Even a huge oak tree with its enormous trunk, hundreds of branches, and thousands of wavy leaves began life as a tiny embryo that continued to grow and grow and grow.

All seed-bearing plants (such as the flowering plants, conifers, cycads, and others) begin life as a tiny embryo wrapped inside a seed that was deposited in the soil under the right conditions. An embryo in plants can be defined as the part of the seed that will develop into the seedling after germination of a fertilized seed. Some seeds are contained within fruits such as apples, tomatoes, and watermelons. Beans, peas, and cantaloupe seeds are all seeds that develop within a fruit. These are known as *angiosperms* and they are the most common group of plants. Other seeds such as those from the trees of cycads, ginkos, and conifers are not contained within a fruit. These are known as *gymnosperms.*

Objective
Determine if potting soil, soil from your backyard, or sand is best at germinating various types of seeds.

Materials
- 12 uncooked bean seeds
- 12 uncooked peas or cantaloupe seeds
- 2 bowls water
- Marker
- 3 disposable plastic cups, 8.5-ounce (250-milliliter) size
- Potting soil
- Fresh, moist soil from your backyard
- 6 ounces (175 grams) sand from a nursery
- Measuring cup
- Notebook
- Ruler

Soak 12 bean seeds in a bowl of water at room temperature overnight. Do the same with 12 pea or cantaloupe seeds. Most seeds will begin to germinate during this time. However, some seeds require seasonal changes, darkness, or a special temperature to begin germination.

Once you have soaked the seeds, label three cups "potting soil," "backyard soil," and "sand." Fill each cup about three-quarters full with the appropriate type of soil. You will plant both types of seeds in each cup. Label one side of each cup with the type of seed you have chosen (bean and peas, for example). Bury four beans about 1 inch (2.5 centimeters) below the surface of the soil of each cup on the appropriate side of the cup. Repeat with four peas or cantaloupe seeds on the other side of the cup. Usually only about half of the seeds will germinate successfully. Add $\frac{1}{4}$ cup of water to your seeds because they require water when they are growing rapidly. Place all of the cups in a warm and sunny place.

Every other day, for the next 4 days, take one seed out of each side of each cup, and then rinse it under running tap water so that you

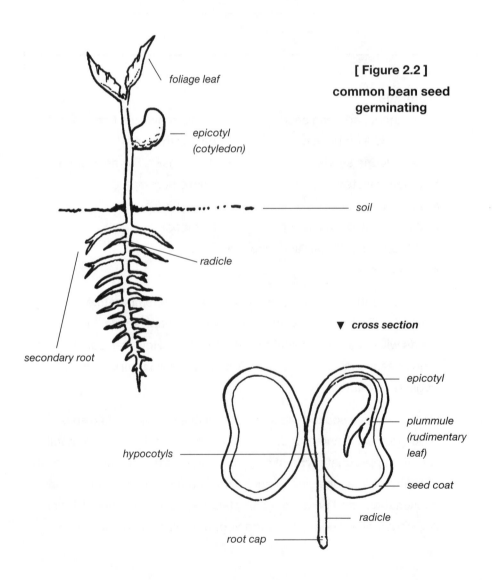

foliage leaf

epicotyl
(cotyledon)

[Figure 2.2]

**common bean seed
germinating**

soil

radicle

▼ **cross section**

secondary root

epicotyl

plummule
(rudimentary
leaf)

hypocotyls

seed coat

radicle

root cap

can measure its growth. For example, if you plant the seeds on Monday, then remove one seed from each pot on Wednesday and again on Friday. Add an additional $\frac{1}{4}$ cup of water to each pot of soil if the soil feels dry to the touch. To measure the growth, rinse the seeds off under running water, then place each seed on a clean surface next to a ruler. Record the length and soil type in a notebook. On day one, you may notice a tiny sprout beginning to exit the seed. The first sprout you will see is the radicle, which becomes the primary root. It develops from a region called the hypocotyl. Next, the stem and leaves will begin to sprout out of the seed. They develop from a region called the epicotyl *(see figure 2.2)*.

Examine the exterior of the seeds for any changes that may have taken place. Look for differences among the seeds as they germinate. Write down your observations in your laboratory notebook so you can refer to them later.

Every plant produces slightly different-looking seeds, but most will have a primary root and one or two temporary structures called cotyledons *(see figure 2.2)*.

Cotyledons are similar to tiny leaves in appearance. The cotyledons are the first sites of photosynthesis, which supplies the new plant with vital nutrients and energy until the leaves emerge. Within a few days, the cotyledons usually wither away. By this time, the true leaves have emerged to take over photosynthesis. Let a few of the seeds continue to sprout all the way out of the soil.

Results

Did the roots or stems grow out of the seeds first? Count how many seeds germinated (sprouted) from each of the different types of soil. Did each soil type have the same number of germinating seeds? If not, which soil type was best (helped produce the most

▶ *The oldest living things on earth today are bristlecone pine trees, which seldom grow to be over 30 feet (9 meters) tall. They live on the west coast of the United States and some are nearly 5,000 years old. Pine trees are capable of staying green all year long in part because their leaves do not give off as much water through the pores called* stoma. *Trees of the genus* Pinus, *to which pine trees belong, form the dominant species in some forests mainly in North America and have great value as lumber and paper.*

germinating seeds) under these conditions? Did you notice a difference among the sizes of the germinated seeds? If so, which soil type helped to produce the longest roots and stems? This is an indication of how well the seeds germinated. Compare the same type of seeds from each type of soil. Is the soil from your backyard, potting soil, or sand the best to plant these types of seeds in?

Variations

Can you think of any other variables that might affect seed germination? Determine if the amount of water you add to seeds in potting soil affects their ability to germinate. Grow eight seeds per pot in two different pots. Water both pots on the first day, then water one of the pots every day for 5 days, but do not water the other pot at all. After 5 days, remove one seed from each pot. Measure the seeds using a ruler and then record the length of the germinating seeds. See if you notice any differences. If you do not notice any differences, continue the experiment for another 2 days while continuing to water only the seeds in one pot. You can also see if temperature has an effect by leaving one pot indoors and the second pot outdoors for a week when the temperature is much hotter or much cooler than it is in your house. Water both pots with ¼ cup of water as needed and place both in a sunny spot.

Growing Grass

Almost all plants need sunlight to survive to fuel the process known as photosynthesis. In this process sunlight provides plants with energy, which they convert into chemical or food energy. Up to a point, the more energy in the form of sunlight provided to the plant, the more it will grow. This will happen until something else limits the growth of the plant, such as the amount of water or nutrients it receives, which can be too much or too little, and even too much sunlight.

The total amount of living plant material, which includes leaves, stems, and roots, in a given area at any given time is called the "standing crop." This is an important measurement because it tells you how much plant material will be available to the rest of the organisms in that community, such as the animals that graze on grass, the insects that consume plants, and the bacteria, fungi, and protozoans that decompose plants.

You can measure the standing crop in 1 square yard (or meter) of your backyard in a sunny location and compare it to a similar plot of grass in a shady location to determine the effect shade has on the grass in your backyard.

Objective

Determine if there is more grass in 1 square yard (or meter) of your backyard in a shady or sunny region. Use this information to estimate the overall aboveground plant products, including grass and weeds, in your entire backyard. Determine if watering a plot of grass that had been previously stripped then reseeded has an effect on the ability of the grass seed to grow back as compared to the control, which has no water added.

Materials

- Yard (or meter) stick
- 8 pencils
- 2 pieces of string, 5 yards (or meters) long
- Garden shovel
- Paper bag

- Bathroom scale (if available)
- Marker
- Notebook
- Grass seeds
- Water bucket

* *Adult supervision recommended*

Locate a shady area in your backyard where your parent(s) or property owner will not mind if you remove the grass from it for a few weeks. Mark off 1 square yard (1 square meter) of grass using a yard (or meter) stick *(see figure 2.3)*.

Do not worry if the patch of grass contains weeds because you will be removing them. Push four pencils into the ground at each corner of the area you are marking off. Use a piece of string to enclose the square by tying the string onto one stick and then wrapping it around the other three pencils in a clockwise fashion, then tying it to the first stick again. Repeat this process for the second square plot of grass in a nearby sunny location.

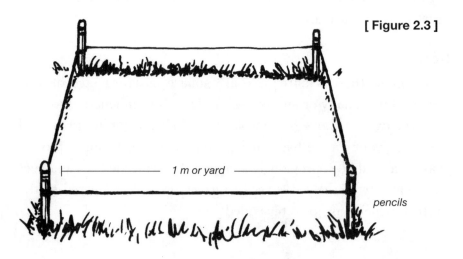

[**Figure 2.3**]

1 m or yard

pencils

Determine the standing crop of grass in the plots you just marked off as follows. Using a garden shovel, remove all of the plants from each of the plots and collect them into a paper bag. Shake as much soil as you can from the roots of the grass back onto the plot you removed it from. Using a marker, label the bags "sunny" and "shady," respectively. Using a scale, weigh the plant material (grass and weeds) in the bag and record the weight, which is the standing crop of 1 square yard (1 square meter). Record your results in your laboratory notebook for later experimentation.

You can use the data collected above to estimate the amount of grass and weeds in your entire backyard. Measure the area of your backyard by multiplying the length by the width of your yard and record the results in your notebook. To do so, count the number of large steps it takes to walk the length then the width of your yard. One large step is about equal to 1 yard (1 meter). Use a yardstick (or meterstick) for the first few steps to get a feeling of how far you should be stepping. Keep stepping so that each step remains equal to 1 yard (1 meter). Remember to keep count as you go and write down your results.

To determine the standing crop of grass in your entire backyard, multiply the area (length x width in meters or yards) of your backyard by the weight of the grass in the sunny plot. Repeat with the weight of the grass in the shady region to compare them. (For example, if you removed 2.2 lbs (1 kilogram) from a previously untouched plot of grass as above: 2.2 pounds (1 kilograms) ÷ 1 square yard [or meter] x 100 yards or meters (steps long) x 50 yards or meters (steps wide) = 11,000 pounds (5,000 kilograms) of grass in your yard, since 1,000 grams = 1 kilogram = 2.2 pounds.) Imagine how much grass there would be if you never cut your grass.

Remove the pencils and string from the shady plots and mark off a second sunny plot next to the first sunny plot you marked off earlier. Measure the effect watering has on two previously stripped plots of grass by stripping a second 1-square-yard (1-square-meter) plot of grass next to the first sunny plot you already stripped. Add grass seed to both plots as follows. Sprinkle 6 ounces (170 grams) of grass seed over the freshly exposed plots of soil. Firmly press on the soil to help bury the seeds in the soil. Water one of the plots of soil by sprinkling 0.5 gallons (2 liters) of water over the soil one or two times a day using a bucket of water. Write down the location of the plot you are going to water in your laboratory notebook. Every day for 1 week, visually compare the two plots to each other as you are watering them. Visually compare the watered plot to the control (not watered) plot to determine which one grew more grass.

Results

How did the standing crop taken from the shady region compare with the sunny region? What does that tell you about the effect sunlight would have on a large area of grass if it were in the shade? Did watering the seeded plot have an effect on the ability of the grass seed to grow? Did any weeds grow in your plots after you seeded them with grass seed? If so, which plot grew more weeds?

Variations

Determine if adding fertilizer to a seeded plot increases the growth of the freshly seeded grass seeds using the method above. Compare the seeded and fertilized plot to a control plot that is seeded but not

▶ *Dandelions are common intruders of lawns and grasses. They were first introduced to America as a garden plant, but quickly became a weed and a pest. The roots were once used to make a substitute for coffee. Some forms of wine are made from the flowers of dandelions. The leaves can be eaten in salads.*

fertilized. Do not water the plots for 24 hours after applying the fertilizer because the fertilizer may be lost to the soil as the water seeps into the soil.

Gravitropism

All seed-bearing plants (such as plants that produce most of the fruits and vegetables that you eat) produce seeds. Seeds are the structures that develop from a fertilized ovule following fertilization in most plants. Examples include watermelon seeds, dandelion seeds, and the seeds found in the core of an apple. They are capable of germinating into a new plant under the right conditions. These conditions vary from plant to plant. But conditions such as water, light, nutrients, and temperature are all major factors.

Have you ever considered gravity an important factor? Gravity is the force that holds you onto the ground. This experiment focuses on a concept fundamental to plant growth, called gravitropism. *Gravitropism* is the ability of organisms, usually plants, to grow in response to gravity. Most plant roots grow toward gravity. This is beneficial because the roots will grow deeply into the soil, allowing the plant to remain upright and collect nutrients and water from the soil. *Positive gravitropism* is when the plant grows toward gravity, or down. *Negative gravitropism* is when the plant grows away from gravity, or up. Both roots and stems can exhibit both forms of gravitropism.

Gravitropism is easy to observe in seeds over a relatively short period of time, making them easy to experiment with. You can determine if field peas respond to gravity and how quickly the response takes. You can also determine whether the response occurs in the root cap (region at the very end of the root).

Objective

Learn about gravitropism to determine if field pea seeds exhibit positive or negative gravitropism. Determine if removing the root cap inhibits the emerging plant's ability to respond to gravity.

Materials
- 10 large, uncooked peas
- Water bowl
- Aluminum foil, 12 inches (30 centimeters) square
- Paper towels
- Duct tape
- Ruler

Soak the peas in a bowl of water at room temperature overnight. This will help the seeds germinate. Place the piece of aluminum foil on a countertop. Put a paper towel on top of the aluminum foil. Fold the paper towel and aluminum foil in half to make a crease similar to the center of a book. Open it back up. Spread the seeds in various orientations along the center of the paper towel.

Add 1 ounce (25 milliliters) of water to the paper towel.

Refold the paper towel along the crease where you placed the seeds. Pat it down so that the seeds are completely covered by the paper towel. Fold the aluminum foil in the same manner and then pinch the three open sides of the aluminum foil so that they will remain closed. The aluminum foil and paper towel should be about 6 inches (15 centimeters) wide and 12 inches (30 centimeters) long at this point. Using a piece of tape, hang the packet above a sink so that if any water drips it will be into the sink. Let the seeds germinate overnight.

Open the packet and inspect the seeds to see if the roots exhibit positive or negative gravitropism. Remove four of the seeds to experiment with the root caps. Rotate the remaining seeds clockwise 90 degrees, then close the packet and hang it in exactly the same orientation as before. Let the seeds grow overnight and then inspect the seeds again. The end of the root will begin to curve if they exhibit positive gravitropism. Do the seeds exhibit positive gravitropism?

Experiment with the root caps of the four seeds that you just removed. At the end of the primary root is a tiny, fingernail-like structure called the root cap. Cells at the root cap contain dense

[Figure 2.4]

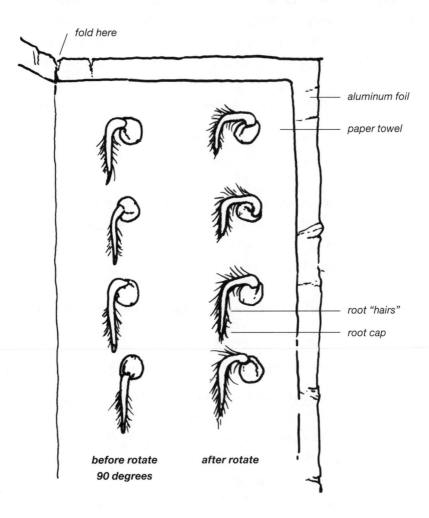

starch granules inside structures called amyloplasts that make the cells heavy. These cells are believed to signal the rest of the root to grow toward the force of gravity. Note the tiny "root hairs," which are actually secondary roots that grow out of the primary root, or radicle *(see figure 2.4)*.

Even if you cannot see the root cap, simply remove the last $\frac{3}{16}$ inch (5 millimeters) of the root from the tip using your fingernail from two of the four seeds, using a ruler to measure it if necessary. Do not remove the root caps from the other two seeds because these will serve as the control batch. Arrange the cut and uncut seeds on a fresh paper towel so that the emerging roots of all four seeds will be facing horizontally (left to right) when they are hanging up as before. Place the paper towel onto a piece of aluminum foil, fold the three open edges, and hang it up as above. Check the seeds the next day.

Results

Did any of the seeds respond to gravity by changing the direction of their growth? Did you notice a difference in the response to gravity between the cut and uncut seeds? Is there something about the root cap that makes seeds respond to gravity? Why do you think gravitropism may be beneficial to the newly emerging plants? What did you notice about the seeds that were rotated 90 degrees?

▶ *Successful reproduction by a seed-bearing plant requires transportation of the seed to a favorable environment. Plants use wind, water, animals, and even forceful ejection to disperse their seeds. The fruit of a coconut may float for weeks in the ocean before reaching the sand of a beach where it may germinate into a coconut tree.*

Variations

Plants can also grow in response to light during a process known as phototropism. The leaves of most plants exhibit positive phototropism, which is when the stems and leaves of a plant grow toward a source of light. However, some plants exhibit negative phototropism. Determine if some common houseplants are positively or negatively phototropic and how long it takes for you to notice the response. Some common plants include *Coleus*, meadow rue, ramosa, Texas tarragon, or Carpathian harebell, which can be purchased at a local nursery or garden shop. Test a commercially purchased ivy plant and compare its response to those of the other houseplants. Carefully pack down the soil in the pot of each plant. If the soil is loose, cover it with aluminum foil around the base of the plant. Set up the experiment by laying the potted plants on their side inside of a shoebox (so that they will not roll over, as well as to block the light from entering on one side) 3 feet (1 meter) in front of a well-lit window or a light source. Return each day for 1 week to determine if the plants respond to the light. Did they respond to light? If so, did they respond positively or negatively? Why do you think this is so?

Test Foods for Starch

Starch is the primary storage molecule of plants. Starch is a *polysaccharide* (complex sugar) made up of two chemical substances called amylose and amylopectin. Starch occurs exclusively in plant cells in the form of granules, which are storage devices used by plants. They are the equivalent of fat cells in humans. Starch is a common component of our diet. Potatoes, wheat, corn, and rice all contain a large amount of starch. Animals ultimately digest or break down starch into smaller molecules of glucose and other storage molecules. Glucose can be modified to be stored as glycogen, the animal form of starch.

Many other plant items contain starch. You can test for the presence of starch using a simple chemical reaction involving iodine. In the presence of starch, elements of iodine stack neatly within the coiled structure of starch. As a result, the iodine-starch complex produces a dark purplish-black color, which you can easily detect visually.

Objective

Learn about a common test for starch, known as the iodine test among scientists, and determine if various foods from your kitchen and backyard contain starch.

Materials

- Green leaves from tree
- Grass clippings
- Potato, scrubbed clean and peeled
- Wheat cereal

- Paper plates
- Sink with running water
- Iodine solution (2 percent is the standard concentration, available at most pharmacies)

✶ *Adult supervision recommended*

Use iodine only under adult supervision. Place some of the leaves, grass, the potato, and wheat cereal onto a paper plate. Place a drop of iodine onto a clean surface of each item *(see figure 2.5)*.

Within 1 minute, the iodine, which is normally light brown, will turn black or deep purple if the item contains starch.

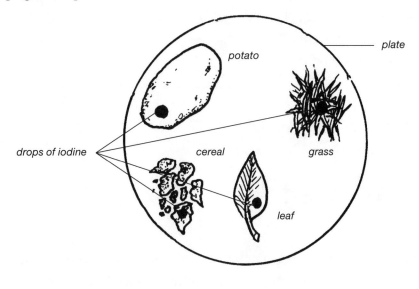

Results

Most plant products you test will contain starch because starch is the major storage molecule for plants. Animals use glycogen molecules to store energy instead of starch so lunch meat, insects, and even worms would test negative for the presence of starch.

Variations

Can you think of any other plant structures that may store starch? Search your backyard for plant items that you feel may contain starch. Test them, too. Before you test each item, try to guess if the item has starch in it. Remember, starch is a storage molecule used to store energy for later use.

▶ *Iodine is found in humans in trace amounts. It is needed for the production of various hormones in the thyroid gland. We ingest minute amounts of iodine, mostly from iodized salt as well as from fish and dairy products.*

Saliva Test

In the previous experiment you discovered how to test items for the presence of starch using a common procedure known among scientists as the iodine test. In this experiment, you can determine if items that are high in starch, such as crackers and rice, get completely broken down into simple sugars over a period of 5 minutes, thereby testing negative according to the iodine test.

Digestion begins as soon as you begin to chew a piece of food and continues for 24–72 hours, until the food item has passed through your digestive tract. Determine if the conversion of a plant product, such as a potato, from a positive to a negative iodine test is due to the action of enzymes, such as amylases, found in saliva. This occurs when the starch in the potato is broken down. Saliva contains water, mucus, and enzymes to aid in the digestion of food. Humans and other *herbivorous* (plant-eating) mammals contain enzymes that can ultimately break down starch into glucose and other simple sugars for energy. This process occurs with the aid of enzymes called amylases. You can determine if the enzymes, which break down as starch, are contained in saliva and if they are capable of breaking down starch within 5 minutes, resulting in a negative iodine test.

Alternatively, you could use Super Papaya Enzymes or a similar brand of papaya enzymes that are available at most pharmacies and health food stores. Papaya enzymes are dietary supplements that contain enzymes similar to those found in your saliva that come from papaya fruit. *Do not eat anything from this experiment.*

Objective

Determine if food items that contain starch test negative for the iodine test before and after they are dissolved in saliva in a plastic cup over a span of 5 minutes.

Materials

- ▶ 1 glass drinking water
- ▶ 1 cup cooked rice
- ▶ Teaspoon
- ▶ Crackers
- ▶ 4 disposable cups
- ▶ 2 disposable cups with 1 ounce (30 milliliters) water
- ▶ Iodine (2 percent solution)

✳ *Adult supervision recommended*

Use iodine only under adult supervision. Rinse your mouth with a small amount of water and spit it out into a plastic cup (or dissolve 1 papaya tablet in some water and replace it with saliva throughout this experiment). Add 1 teaspoon of rice to the cup of saliva so that the enzymes in saliva can digest it for about 5 minutes. Using a spoon, crush the rice and mix it with the saliva. Remove some of the rice using the spoon and test it using a small drop of iodine. Test rice that was not dissolved in the saliva in another cup for comparison. As a control, test the same amount of rice that was dissolved in water for several minutes.

Repeat the process with the same amount of crackers and a fresh cup of saliva and water. Did the digestive enzymes in your saliva break down the starch and result in a negative iodine test after 5 minutes?

Results

Crackers and rice, which contain starch, should test positive for starch before the addition of the saliva. However, after the addition of the saliva, they should test negative because the enzymes in saliva should break the starch down into simple sugars that do not test positive for starch. The crackers and rice dissolved in water should test positive for the presence of starch because they will not be broken down into simple sugars. Is this what you found? If not, try again but soak the items for 30 minutes.

▶ *Many insects contain digestive enzymes in their saliva. The saliva of blood-sucking insects such as mosquitoes contain anticoagulants, which halt blood clotting, thus helping them to obtain more blood.*

Carnivorous Plants

Carnivorous plants seem to generate more interest than all of the other members of the plant kingdom combined. Carnivorous plants, or "CPs" for short, are a group of plants so strange that they could have come right out of a science fiction movie. Most plants and animals are constantly bothered by insects and other pests. CPs actually do something about it. They have evolved to be able to digest insects and other pests for food. Like all other plants, CPs still undergo photosynthesis as a means of converting solar energy into chemical or food energy, but they also indulge on insects whenever the opportunity arises. Some can even eat a thousand insects or more in their lifetime.

The American pitcher plant is found all along the East Coast, ranging as far north as Canada to as far south as Florida. They are the easiest CPs to grow and maintain inside as well as outdoors. The Venus's-flytrap is another fascinating CP. They look like small clams with huge fanglike teeth separated with gaps between them. As you will see, these two plants capture insects by similar, yet different, means.

Often in biology, the most important thing you can do is simply observe an organism. In this experiment, observing CPs is as informative and interesting as experimenting with them. Once you have learned the secrets to successfully growing CPs, you will be able to experiment and study them for years. You can grow CPs from seeds; however, that would take one or two seasons. Therefore, the best way to grow CPs is to obtain them from a grower that has started the process for you.

Objective

Learn how to grow CPs or other plants in a terrarium, discover how they capture and feed off prey such as insects, and observe them as they feed on insects.

Materials

- Scissors
- 1-gallon (4-liter) plastic milk carton
- Plastic sandwich bag
- Tape
- Sand
- Sink
- Water
- Peat moss or sphagnum moss (available from a local plant supply store or nursery)
- Venus's-flytrap and/or American pitcher plant (available from a nursery or see list of resources at the end of this book)
- 1 gallon (4 liters) distilled water
- Fluorescent (fish tank or greenhouse) light

One of the most important factors when growing CPs is humidity. To ensure that your CP will have enough humidity, you will need to create a plant container that has a small opening at the top as well as adding a clear lid to it that will allow sunlight to pass through. To do this, you can put the entire plant and pot in a terrarium or a 1-gallon (4-liter) plastic or glass fishbowl. You can also modify a milk carton to make the opening large enough for you to fit the plants into it. The narrow opening also serves to keep the moisture or humidity in *(see figure 2.6)*.

Using a pair of scissors, cut open a 1-gallon (4-liter) milk carton from the top opening about 4 inches (10 centimeters) down and all the way around *(see figure 2.6)*. A container such as this one used for houseplants is commonly referred to as a terrarium.

Create a lid by using a clear sandwich bag. Hang the baggie over the opening and secure it on one side using a piece of tape so that you can open and close it easily to feed and water your plants. Alternatively, if the plant is potted, you can place the entire plant and

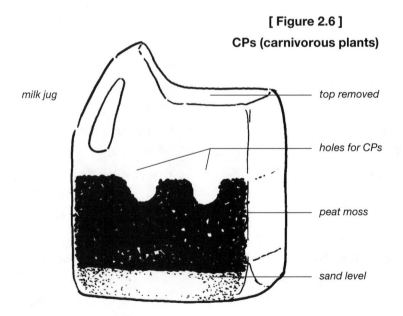

[Figure 2.6]
CPs (carnivorous plants)

milk jug

top removed

holes for CPs

peat moss

sand level

pot in a sealed plastic bag with a few holes poked into it so that it can get fresh air. This will maintain the moisture while still allowing sunlight to get in.

Once your plants arrive, you will have to replant them in the appropriate type of soil and the right size pot. Save any soil that came with the plants and use it to replant them. Both types of CPs are accustomed to growing in sand and peat moss. Rinse the sand with running tap water for 1–2 minutes to remove any minerals that might be present. Repeat with the peat moss or sphagnum moss. Drain the sand and then rinse it again with distilled water to remove the minerals in the tap water.

Add a 2-inch (5-centimeter) layer of sand at the bottom of the milk carton. Overlay the sand with enough of the peat moss or sphagnum moss to fill the container halfway to the top. The larger the container, the more sand and moss you will have to add. Dig a separate hole about 1 inch (2.5 centimeters) deep for each plant to fit into. Gently place the roots of the CP down into the moss. Carefully place some more moss around the base of the plant. The plant's roots will soon grow into the moss and stabilize itself. Add enough mineral-free water to your plants so that the moss and sand are quite damp. Cover the opening of the container with the plastic bag you taped to the side of the container.

When watering your CPs, do not let the water level reach the roots or they may rot. Remember, CPs are sensitive to the type of water you use, so use distilled water that is free of minerals. You will notice that the moss is very absorbent, so your CP will not have any difficulty getting water from this environment.

Open the bag every other day, or poke a few holes in the top of the bag, to allow fresh air to get in. CPs need 12–16 hours of light per day. Place them somewhere that they will receive a lot of natural or fluorescent light such as on a window ledge or in your bathroom or kitchen. If you have a fluorescent light, place it somewhere near your CPs to give them plenty of light but not overheat them. If the water evaporates within 3–4 days, you are giving them too much artificial light, so move the light farther away.

You can stimulate the Venus's-flytrap into closing its trap by gently yet rapidly flicking one side of the trap five or six times. This will mimic a fly getting trapped in its trap. The trap will spring shut in the blink of an eye so be sure not to miss it. Try this after putting a dead insect in the trap that you found in your backyard and see what happens to it after a week or so.

Results

When CPs were first discovered in the 1700s, many scientists did not believe the plants were actually eating the insects. Were you able to demonstrate for yourself that the plants really do eat the insects and that the insects are not just decomposing naturally? Feed your CPs and document what happens in your laboratory notebook.

Place your CPs outside on a warm summer day and remove the lid. See how long it takes your CPs to capture food on their own. Can you tell how insects are attracted to your CP and how the excrement (what remains of the insect that the plant does not use) is removed by observing them? How might the remaining insect debris be removed in the wild as opposed to in your terrarium? Do you think that wind and rain may play a role?

> ▶ *Carnivorous plants eat insects, spiders, and sow bugs to gain valuable nutrients such as nitrogen, phosphorous, and potassium. Rare, larger CPs have been known to eat organisms as large as frogs and rats.*

Variations

CPs require insects to obtain essential nutrients. Do you think it is because they grow in soil that is void of these nutrients, or because they need a lot more of them? Grow CPs in different types of soil. Grow one CP in the soil mentioned above, a second in ordinary plant soil, and a third in ordinary plant soil with fertilizer added to it. The best way to apply fertilizer to CPs is to actually spray or spread a liquid fertilizer over the leaves. CPs do not have an extensive root system like many other plants, largely because they are accustomed to growing in damp, sandy soil.

Species

A *species* is often defined as a group of organisms that are capable of producing fertile offspring together. It is often easy to distinguish between two different species of animals because they look entirely different. It is safe to say that a human, a sponge, and an ant are all members of three different species simply by their appearance. However, it is not so easy with plants. At first glance, many plants look remarkably similar. But if you take a closer look at things such as the size of their leaves, the number of branches on an adult tree, and the appearance of their seeds, you will see that it becomes easier to distinguish different species of plants.

Objective

Estimate the number of leaves and the total leaf area of four different types of trees and compare them.

Materials

- ▶ Marker
- ▶ Label tape
- ▶ 4 plastic sandwich bags
- ▶ Graph paper
- ▶ Calculator (optional)
- ▶ Notebook
- ▶ Scissors
- ▶ Ruler
- ▶ Bowl

Find four trees with differently shaped leaves that are about the same size as one another. Common trees with leaves that will work well include oak, maple, and pine trees. Try to pick an assortment of trees so that you can compare the results.

Using a marker and some label tape, label a plastic bag for each tree you wish to collect leaves from with the common name of that particular tree. If you do not know the name of the tree, give it a descriptive label such as "tall tree with large, flat, pointy leaves." Remember the location of the trees for future reference.

Collect 10 leaves that are green and healthy, not brown and brittle, and place them in the appropriately labeled bag. Approximate the number of leaves on one branch of each of the trees you selected, and then make a note of it in your laboratory notebook. Next, approximate the number of branches on each of the trees as follows. Look at one branch that has fallen on the ground or that is close enough to the ground that you can see and note how many tiny branches are on one major branch. Do not climb the tree. Estimate the number of major branches by looking at the tree and counting as many as you can see. This does not have to be extremely accurate; an estimate will do.

Label the graph paper with the name on the plastic bag. Trace the perimeter of three average-size leaves from the same plastic bag onto the graph paper with a marker. The sizes of leaves will vary somewhat within the same tree *(see figure 2.7)*.

[Figure 2.7]

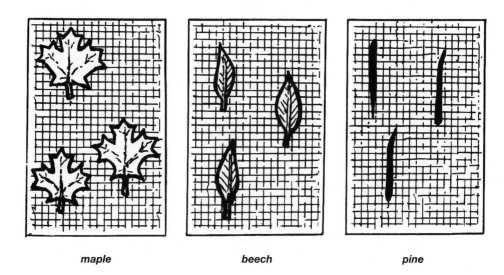

maple   beech   pine

Do not use leaves that are unusually large or small because this may skew your results. Count the number of whole, large squares (not the tiny squares) that are within the traced area for each leaf and then multiply that number by the area of each square. Note: standard graph paper can be purchased with either 1-centimeter or $\frac{1}{2}$-inch squares corresponding to 1 square centimeter ($\frac{1}{4}$ square inch) respectively. For example, if you counted nine squares (3 x 3) from a maple leaf, that would equal 9 square centimeters, if you were using graph paper with square centimeters. This number is the total area of one leaf.

Now you can determine the total surface area of the entire tree by multiplying that number by the total number of leaves estimated earlier. Do this calculation on the same piece of graph paper and save it for future use. Determine the total number of leaves on the tree by multiplying the estimated number of major branches by the estimated number of small branches by the number of leaves per branch by the area of one leaf (*see graph below*). You will be able to compare different kinds of trees using this number.

LEAF NAME	MAPLE	BEECH	PINE	UNKNOWN IN YARD
1. Number of small branches/ major branch	150	110	15	22
2. Number of leaves/branch	20	25	150	45
3. Number of major branches	50	45	25	25
4. Area of leaf	5	6	0.5	4
Total area = 1 x 2 x 3 x 4	750,000	742,500	28,125	99,000

Compare your results from each of the four different trees. Compare the number of branches, number of leaves, and total surface area of the leaves. Trees with different values are probably different species. You should be able to look at a variety of trees and more easily determine if they are members of a different species.

Results

Did you notice any differences between the different species of trees? What type of tree had the most number of leaves? What type of tree had the greatest area of leaves? Did you expect to see a different result? You may wish to compare the areas of the leaves from two vastly different plants such a tree versus a bush using the method in this experiment. Which do you think has more leaves per branch, branches per tree, and total surface area of leaves per plant, a tree or a bush?

> ▶ *It is estimated that 80 percent of our food comes from six species of plants; 95 percent comes from just 20 species. Tea and coffee are the world's most popular beverages, and both are made from plants. Unfortunately, many children are poisoned each year from eating wild plants, so never eat a plant growing in the wild.*

3

Animals That Fly, Walk, and Wiggle

(Kingdom Animalia)

When you think of the word *animals*, dogs, rabbits, and birds are all creatures that may come to mind. Animals belong to the kingdom Animalia. The animal kingdom is composed of a variety of organisms ranging from those just mentioned to insects, worms, spiders, sponges, and, of course, humans.

All living things have a great deal in common with one another, which makes defining them difficult. However, all animals can be defined as multicellular (many-celled) living organisms that obtain energy usually by ingestion (eating other organisms whole or in parts) and arise from the fertilization of an egg cell by a sperm cell.

Animals are fun to observe because they have many unusual habits and unique capabilities. For example, sponges and worms are capable of regenerating lost body parts; ticks, ants, and other animals communicate with one another using chemicals called pheromones; and spiders build amazing webs out of silk. Insects are especially interesting because they can fly, hop, jump, and swim. They often work together in groups and react predictably in many situations. Insects are one of the most diverse groups of animals known to humans. They inhabit the land, air, and sea, where they are capable of eating plants, parts of animals, and other insects along the way.

Ant Food

Insects have three pairs of legs, one pair of antennae, and a hard shell made of a complex sugar called *chitin*. Spiders have four sets of legs; therefore, they are not insects but arachnids. The body of a typical insect has a head, thorax (body), and abdomen (rear) *(see figure 3.1)*.

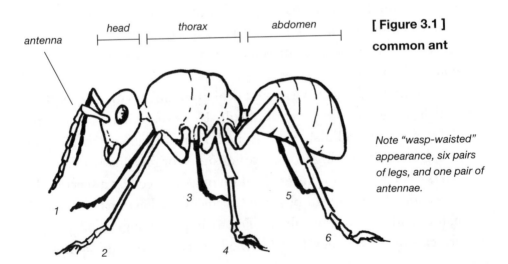

antenna

head   thorax   abdomen

[Figure 3.1]
common ant

Note "wasp-waisted" appearance, six pairs of legs, and one pair of antennae.

1   2   3   4   5   6

Insects have special receptors for taste, which are usually located on their head near the mouth, and receptors for smell, which are usually located on the antennae. The receptors contain specialized cells called *seta*, the plural of which is *setae*. Insects can distinguish between different food substances using their setae.

Do you think ants and other insects have favorite foods? In this experiment, you can try to determine what foods they are most attracted to. You can also watch how ants search for and gather food. This experiment is most fun performed during the summer months when insects are more active.

Objective

Learn how insects use complex senses such as their ability to smell and taste to locate food. Determine if ants are most attracted to syrup, sugar, rice, or salt. Determine if dissolving the same items in water increases or decreases the time it takes for ants to locate them.

Materials
- 1 sheet of thick paper, $8\frac{1}{2}$ x 11 inches
- Glue
- 5 disposable cups, 3.4-ounce (100-milliliter) size
- Sugar
- Salt
- Maple syrup
- Empty cardboard shoebox
- Watch
- Magnifying glass

Tear the sheet of paper into five equal pieces. Add one drop of glue to the center of each piece of paper. Place one side of each paper cup onto the drop of glue on the paper. The paper will help weigh the cup down and keep it from rolling (see figure 3.2).

Place a small amount of sugar, rice, salt, and maple syrup into its own cup so that you can determine which one the insects are most

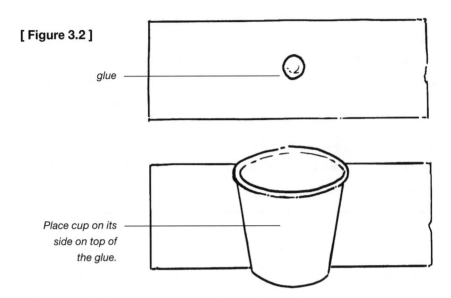

[Figure 3.2]

glue

Place cup on its
side on top of
the glue.

attracted to. Leave one cup empty as a control. Place the cups upright in a shoebox and take them outside.

Locate an anthill. Start by looking in your backyard. There should be several different kinds of ants even in your own backyard. Most ants will work fine. However, fire ants found in the southeastern United States (from Texas to North Carolina) have a stinging bite, so you should avoid them. They are shiny and black with hairlike projections from their arms and legs.

Try to experiment with several anthills, if you locate more than one. A good place to look is near a sidewalk. If you do not find any there, try against the side of your house. Gently place each cup on its side, paper side touching the ground, about 3 feet (1 meter) from the anthill and observe what happens. The ants should go to the food they are most attracted to first. Set your watch to see how long it takes for the ants to locate the food source. Insects are usually very quick to locate the food using their setae. However, it may take up to an hour depending on how many insects there are in the area, the strength of the wind, and your choice of food. The ants will eventually locate the food and appear to show a preference for one. Notice whether they have to sample each cup including the control (empty) cup before they determine which contains their favorite food or whether they go right to one cup. Count how many ants go to each cup and if they go to one cup first.

Use a magnifying glass to study the ants. Ants, wasps, and bees can be distinguished from other insects by their two sets of wings (most ants lose their wings early in life), their long antennae, well-developed eyes, and "wasp-waisted" appearance, created by where the thorax connects to the abdomen. Keep an eye on the food because insects are not the only animals that may be attracted to it.

Results

Which food did the ants feed from first and most often? Scientists think that insects such as the blowfly, which mainly feed on dead animals, respond to meat and salt to the greatest extent. However, insects respond to a variety of tastes, and they perceive these tastes with several different types of receptors.

▶ *Scientists have discovered and identified more species of insects than any other group of animals to date. Worldwide, scientists have discovered over 500,000 species of beetles and weevils (of the order Coleoptera) alone. In fact, insects outnumber all other identified species of plants and animals combined. However, no animals are more unusual than the sponges, which must filter an estimated 1 ton of water to filter enough food to grow just 1 ounce (30 grams). Sponges are also interesting animals because they are* sessile *(not free to move around) and come in a great diversity of colors and shapes. Some of the bright colors seen in sponges are due to algae living inside the sponge.*

Living Garbage Disposal

Does your family recycle any of its waste? If not, you should consider it because recycling is a great way to protect the environment from the accumulation of too much waste. In nature, living organisms are constantly recycling dead and dying tissue during a process called *decomposition*. Bacteria and fungi are the most important organisms in decomposition, especially in soil. They help to break down complex organic compounds, such as protein and carbohydrates, into simpler ones that can be absorbed by plants and other microorganisms.

Without decomposition, dead material such as leaves would begin to accumulate. If the material on a forest floor did not decompose, the leaves on the ground eventually would form a pile as tall as the trees. Decomposition makes nitrogen and other essential elements available to plants by breaking down the leaves and other dead plant and animal debris.

Composting is a form of decomposition and a way to recycle your food waste while also increasing the fertility of the soil that you use to grow plants in or around your home. Bacteria and fungi in soil play a huge role during composting. Worms can play an important part in this process as well. Worms speed up the process of decomposition by eating their way through leaf litter and other decomposing plant material so that the bacteria and fungi can continue the process more easily. During composting, worms burrow through the soil and leave it in better condition than when they found it. When worms eat their way through soil, nutrients are extracted from the soil and the material that is left behind is called a *cast*. As a result, the soil becomes tilled and the fertility of the soil is increased.

Objective

Learn how to recycle old food scraps by composting and determine if the rate of decomposition is greater due to the addition of live worms by building two living garbage disposals, one with worms and the other without.

Materials

- 2 large plastic containers, 10-gallon (40-liter) size
- Mild detergent
- Screwdriver
- Plastic garbage bag
- Vermiculite (available from a plant supply shop)
- Bucket
- Shovel
- 8 buckets of soil from your backyard
- 16 drinking straws
- 4 dozen live worms—black worms, night crawlers, or red worms (red wigglers) [available at tackle shops or see the resources section to find out how to have them shipped directly to you]
- Notebook
- Marker

Soak two plastic containers overnight in water containing a mild detergent. This will remove any harsh chemicals in the plastic that might be harmful to the worms. Rinse the containers thoroughly with warm water.

Poke 10 holes in the bottom of the plastic containers with a screwdriver. Repeat with each of the lids. Place the containers outdoors on top of a plastic garbage bag.

Add vermiculite to the bottom of the containers until it reaches 2 inches (5 centimeters) in depth. Vermiculite is a porous substance often used in worm composting because it increases the flow of air into the soil and allows moisture to accumulate. Collect eight buckets of soil from your backyard using a garden shovel or purchase potting soil from a nursery. Add four buckets of soil to each container. Push eight straws straight down into the soil of each container *(see figure 3.3).*

The straws will allow fresh air, which contains oxygen, to enter the soil. The straws will also allow carbon dioxide gas to escape. Add one bucket of water to each container.

Add four dozen worms to one container. In a notebook, record which container contains the worms. (Be gentle with the worms because they are delicate living creatures.) Then replace the lids on each container.

Bacteria and fungi decompose just about anything. But worms do not ingest just any garbage. They are vegetarians, which means they do not ingest meat. They cannot ingest fatty foods like fast food or dairy products either. They love vegetables such as lettuce, spinach, potatoes, and broccoli.

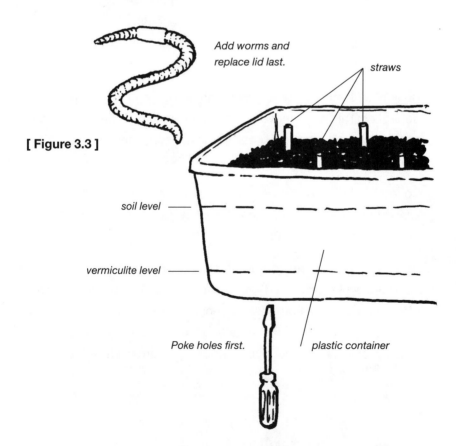

Add worms and replace lid last.

straws

[Figure 3.3]

soil level

vermiculite level

Poke holes first.

plastic container

Collect food to add to your disposal such as apple cores, orange peels, and lettuce. Leaves from your backyard make a great addition, too. Add an equal amount of each item to both containers. Make a note of everything that you add to the containers so that you can determine how much food each container is able to decompose. For starters, add one handful of food to your living garbage disposal per week. These should function without any assistance and should be kept outside. Remember to add food and water every few days. You may have to add less food to one of the containers if you notice it is not able to keep up with the other one. Write down in your notebook how much you added to each container. When adding the food, bury it at least 4 inches (10 centimeters) below the surface of the soil so the worms can get to it and so that it will not smell bad.

You will have to determine how often to provide fresh food to your worms. If they have not finished ingesting what you previously fed them, do not add any more food until it is mostly gone. If a food item remains undigested, remove it. Add two cups of water to your disposal every few days. Only add water if the soil just below the surface feels dry to the touch because you might drown the worms. The soil should be moist, but not soaked.

Once a month, you can harvest the fertile soil and then redistribute it to your houseplants, garden, put it back where you found it, or use it in the experiments below. The soil collected from the living garbage disposal is very fertile and plants will love it.

Results

Which container has a faster rate of decomposition (is able to decompose the food more quickly)? Why do you think this is so? Where do your worms "hang out" the most? Do they clump together or stay apart? Save the freshly composted soil and add it

> ▶ *Everything in Australia seems to be bigger. For example, the largest worm is the giant Australian earthworm. It can grow to be 9 feet (3 meters) long. Australia is also home to giant termites that build huge nests up to 20 feet (6 meters) in height.*

to the soil below your favorite tree in your backyard. When you are finished with your living garbage disposals, release the worms somewhere they can live such as in your backyard, in the woods, or in a park where they will help to aerate the soil for the plants.

Trapping Flying Insects

When most people think of flying insects, the housefly, deerfly, mosquito, beetle, and bee may come to mind. Other people might think of the butterfly, firefly (lightning bug), or cricket. Regardless of which insects you think of, the more closely you study insects, the more you will want to learn about them. Trapping insects is easiest when the outside temperature is above 77°F (22°C) because that is when insects are most active.

Objective
Collect insects that fly both during the day and at night so that you can investigate if they differ in size, shape, wingspan, or appearance. Compare how many insects you can capture at night versus during the day.

Materials

- ► Large cardboard box
- ► Scissors
- ► Duct tape
- ► Pencil
- ► 2 pieces of twine

- ► Marker
- ► 4 glass jars with lids
- ► Magnifying glass
- ► 2 sheets of white paper
- ► Notebook

Cut out a square piece of cardboard 1 yard (1 meter) long by 1 yard (1 meter) wide from a large cardboard box. Fold the flat piece of cardboard along one edge 2 inches (5 centimeters) from the bottom *(see figure 3.4)*.

Use duct tape to secure the fold in place at a 45 degree angle from the rest of the cardboard. This will serve as a gutter for the dead insects to fall into after they fly into the cardboard.

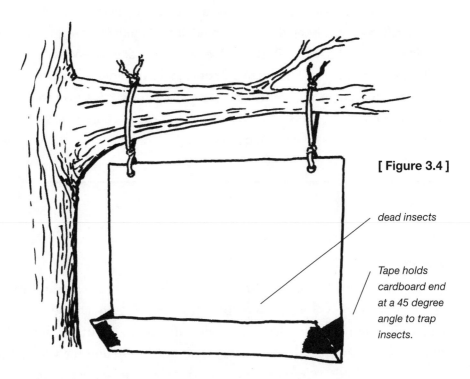

[Figure 3.4]

dead insects

Tape holds cardboard end at a 45 degree angle to trap insects.

Poke two holes in the top of the cardboard about 1 foot (30 centimeters) apart and 1 inch (2.5 centimeters) from the edge using a pencil. Thread each hole with a piece of twine about 1 foot (30 centimeters) long. Label four jars "backyard," "backyard night," "woods," and "woods night." In the morning, hang the cardboard from a tree and wait to collect insects. Wait 8 hours, and then collect the insects that fly into the cardboard and fall into the gutter below by dumping them into the jar labeled "backyard" and close the lid.

Repeat this process in a nearby park so that you can determine if you can trap more insects in your backyard or a nearby park. Save these insects in the jar labeled "woods." Collect the insects after the same amount of time in both locations so that you can accurately compare them. Collecting at least 10 insects from each location should take no more than 4 days to achieve. Determine if there are more insects in the same locations at night by setting up the trap in the evening, then collecting the insects the next morning using the other two jars.

Count and examine the insects from all four jars by using a magnifying glass. Keep them separated. Insects that fly at night are different than those that fly during the day. Look for differences between the two. Do insects that fly at night have larger or smaller eyes? On average, are night insects larger or smaller? Are their wings longer or shorter? Write your observations down in a notebook so you can compare all of the information.

Results

From your own experience, do insects make more noise at night or during the day? Why do you think this is so? Can you identify which insects make noise? Try to identify the parts of the insect that make the noise. Most insects make noise by rubbing various parts of their body together. Try to notice the unusual openings on

▶ *Beetles arose some 250 million years ago but only flourished with the advent of flowering plants some 100 million years ago because of their ability to feed on the leaves, cones, and flowers of these plants. The common American grasshopper (*Schistocerca americana*) can be found as large as 4 inches (10 centimeters) long when fully grown. Unlike humans, insects such as the grasshopper rely on an exoskeleton (a supportive shell) to support the weight of their body, thereby limiting the size of their growth.*

the belly of some night-flying insects. What do you think the holes are for?

Trapping Grasshoppers and Crickets

In addition to trapping flying insects, you can trap insects that crawl and hop as well. Crickets and grasshoppers are closely related insects belonging to the order called Orthoptera by scientists. Crickets and grasshoppers are good to study because they are easy to trap alive and can be easily released where you found them. Although crickets and grasshoppers are usually found on the ground, they are able to fly, and they are especially interesting because of the interesting chirping noises they make, which are commonly used to attract a mate or to scare away other males.

Adult crickets and grasshoppers are most commonly found in tall grass during the late summer and early fall months. You do not need to distinguish between the two in this experiment; however, true grasshoppers (family Acrididae) generally have antennae that are shorter than their body, while crickets (family Gryllidae) often have antennae that are at least as long as their body.

Objective

Determine if there are more crickets and grasshoppers in an area of your backyard or a nearby park with short or long grass.

Materials

- Yard (or meter) stick
- 4 pencils
- String
- 2 butterfly nets (or an old bed sheet and old tennis racket if you would prefer to make one)
- Clear glass jar with lid
- A partner
- Laboratory notebook
- Pen

This experiment works best in the late summer or early fall when the crickets and grasshoppers are most active. Determine how many crickets and/or grasshoppers there are in 1 square yard (or meter) of grass in your backyard as follows. Choose two plots of grass, one that is uncut and undisturbed such as in a field or park and a second that is mowed regularly such as in your backyard. Mark off a 1-yard- (or meter-) square plot using a yard (or meter) stick in each area. Push 4 pencils into the ground at each corner of the area you are marking off. Enclose the square using a piece of string by tying the string onto one pencil and then wrapping it around the other 3 pencils in a clockwise fashion and then tie it off. Repeat this at the second location (see figure 3.5).

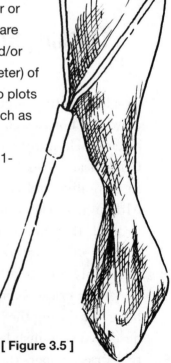

[Figure 3.5]

Return to the plots the next day because you may have disturbed some of the insects while marking off the areas. Using a butterfly net, rake the grass from the edge of the plot toward the center. Your partner should do the same from the opposite side of the plot so that you are both raking the grass with your nets toward the center of the plot. This is to ensure that most of the crickets and grasshoppers do not escape.

If you cannot borrow a butterfly net from your home or school, you can make one using an old bed sheet and an old tennis racket. Cut out a large circle about 1 yard (1 meter) in diameter from the center of the bed sheet. Cut out the strings from an old tennis racket and attach the bed sheet to it using duct tape.

Grab the crickets and grasshoppers one at a time from the net and then quickly place them into a glass jar with a lid. You will be able to observe them better in the clear glass jar than in the net. Replace the lid every time you add a new insect so that the others do not escape. Once you and your partner have raked the entire plot of grass and believe you have collected all the crickets and grasshoppers in that plot of grass, count them and then release them back into the center of the plot of grass. Repeat the measurement at the second plot immediately after the first so that you are making your counts at about the same time without any temperature or light change, which can effect your results. Record your results in your laboratory notebook.

Results

Which plot had more crickets and grasshoppers? You may want to repeat the experiment to be sure you sampled them accurately. Determine how many crickets and grasshoppers there are in your entire backyard by multiplying this number, which is the amount of

▶ *Grasshoppers and other insects belong to the phylum Arthropoda, of which there are over 1 million species. Grasshoppers and other insects have tiny muscles attached to the inside of their exoskeleton. The muscles in the relatively long hind legs of grasshoppers are unique in that they act like powerful levers, allowing them to jump at an astonishing 3.5 meters per second.*

crickets and grasshoppers in 1 square meter, by the length and width of your backyard, which you can calculate as follows. Measure the area of your backyard by multiplying the length by the width of your yard and record the results in your notebook. To do so, count the number of large steps it takes to walk the length and then the width of your yard. One large step is about equal to 1 yard (1 meter). Use a yard (or meter) stick for the first few steps to get a feeling of how far you should be stepping. Then keep stepping so that each step remains equal to 1 yard (1 meter). Write down your results.

Spider Webs

Why are so many people afraid of spiders? Perhaps it is because of their unusual shape, vivid colors, mysterious behavior, or bad reputation. Spiders, ticks, scorpions, horseshoe crabs, and dust mites are commonly known as arachnids. Arachnids are very similar to insects in that they have jointed appendages, an outer shell or exoskeleton made of protein and the compound *chitin* (which is a complex sugar), segmented bodies, and similar habitats. Spiders are distinctly different from insects, however. Spiders have four pairs of legs (insects have three pairs). Spiders also have a pair of pedipalps that look like a fifth pair of legs, and many produce intricate webs of silk often used to capture prey. The bodies of spiders are divided into two segments called the abdomen and cephalothorax, whereas insects have three segments (head, thorax, and abdomen), and spiders do not have wings or antennae as insects do.

You will capture and nurture spiders in this experiment. Once captured, you will allow the spiders to spin their webs and examine this process in close detail. No two spiders make the same web design, but there are three main types of webs that you should look for: orb, sheet, and funnel. Orb webs resemble a traditional Spiderman web, sheet webs are flat like a piece of paper, and a tunnel web looks like the opening to a cave. The webs are made of silk, and the spinnerets, located at the rear of the spider, are where the silk comes out. Not all spiders make webs. The jumping spider does not catch its prey in a web but jumps on them. The Carolina wolf spider sneaks up on its prey, which can be hard to accomplish because they are one of the largest spiders, ranging from 0.9 to 1.4 inches (25 to 35 millimeters) in length.

One common spider found across the United States is the orb weaver spider, also known as the garden spider. The garden spider is black and yellow and is commonly found in tall grass and near dead tree branches and leaves. Other common spiders include the funnel web spider, also known as the grass spider, which is commonly seen in the morning when the dew makes its webs more noticeable, and the daddy longlegs. The most poisonous spiders are the black widow, brown recluse, and the Australian funnelweb.

Objective

Capture some spiders to observe them make webs out of silk. Determine what type of web they make: orb, sheet, or funnel.

Materials

- 2 glass jars, about 1-quart (0.5-liter) size, with lids
- 2 thin twigs, 3 inches (8 centimeters) in length
- Dried leaves
- Cheesecloth or a piece of cloth
- Rubber bands

With a jar and lid in hand, begin your search for spiders. They are most active during daylight hours when they are out looking for prey or working on their web. Carefully capture one spider per jar by flicking it into the open jar using a twig or stick. Immediately cap the jar. Once you have gathered the spiders you wish to study, you will have to add the twigs and some leaves to your jars. The twigs should be long enough to stand almost upright in the jar so that the spider will spin its web on them. Do not let the spider escape. However, keep in mind that spiders need oxygen (air) to breathe, so replace the lid with a piece of cheesecloth and carefully secure it onto the jar using a rubber band.

Place the jar somewhere safe and out of direct sunlight for a few days to allow the spider to go to work on its web. Remember to feed your spider; crickets or beetles will make a hearty meal for most spiders.

Each day, watch as the spider spins its web. You will notice that once the spider begins its web, it works nearly nonstop—as if it were obsessed with getting it finished. Different spiders make unique patterns in their webs. If you collected multiple spiders, they may make different webs. Can you notice a difference? Inspect the web at various stages during its construction. What did you notice?

▶ *Spiders are members of the group of insects known as arachnids, which comes from the name of the taxonomical class Arachnida, to which they belong. Most arachnids are terrestrial (live on land) and are carnivorous (meat-eaters). The Eurasian water spider is the only spider that lives, eats, and lays its eggs totally under water. It collects air from the surface and deposits it in the form of air bubbles beneath its underwater web and breathes from those bubbles whenever it needs oxygen.*

4

There Is a Fungus Among Us

(Kingdom Fungi)

Mushrooms, yeast, and mold are members of the kingdom Fungi. Fungi are predominately found living in the ground in the form of microscopic hyphae where they come together to form a more complex structures called mycelia. However, they can also be found on fruits, vegetables, foods such as jelly, and even on you. For example, athlete's foot is a common name for a kind of fungus that feeds off the skin most commonly found between your toes.

Fungi are of great importance to the environment due to the process of decomposition as discussed in relation to bacteria in chapter 1. Fungi are a unique group of organisms that resemble both plants and animals. However, they are neither.

Fungi differ from plants in a variety of ways. Fungi do not contain chlorophyll and they do not perform photosynthesis, therefore they are not plants. Most fungi obtain nutrients (food) by extracting them off dead or dying plant and animal debris. This is known as *saprophytic*. Other fungi are *parasitic*, which means they feed off plants or animals that are still living.

Unlike the majority of higher plants (trees, flowers, and shrubs, for example), most fungi are capable of reproducing asexually, whereas most plants generally do not. (Notable plant exceptions include aspens, dandelions, strawberries, the spider plant, and cholla cacti.) Fungi undergo asexual reproduction by means of spores, budding (mainly in yeast), and fragmentation, or the breaking apart of hyphae. Fungal spores are tiny, asexual reproductive cells. If a fungal spore lands on a suitable place to grow, it will produce hyphae.

Some complex fungi produce mushrooms. Mushrooms are actually a dense mass of mycelia commonly called a basidiocarp, sporophore, or fruiting body. The fruiting body is the part of the mushroom that is commonly seen growing out of the ground.

Mushrooms are the most commonly known fungi. Mushrooms are often cultivated for food in dark cellars, caves, or greenhouses. They are also grown in laboratories for medicine. In natural settings, mushrooms pop up after they have stored adequate nutrients and when the moisture level in the soil is sufficient. They often appear in the same location year after year, making it easy to predict where they will turn up. Many mushroom are poisonous, so never touch a wild mushroom.

Yeast are a form of fungi. They are unicellular and reproduce mainly by budding. They are important in the baking and brewing industries. They are also found on crops such as fruits and vegetables, contaminating them.

Yeast Metabolism

Yeast are microscopic, single-celled fungi found naturally in soil and on plants and fruits, where they appear as a white powdery coat. Yeast cells absorb nutrients from the environment for energy and growth. During this process, the yeast takes in complex compounds such as sugar, carbohydrates, and protein and *metabolizes* (breaks down) the compounds into simpler ones such as pyruvate, sugars, and amino acids. Ultimately, this metabolization produces carbon dioxide. A similar process also occurs in your body. However, rather than metabolizing it, you exhale carbon dioxide from specialized organs called lungs.

By supplying yeast cells with sugar while they are dissolved in warm water, you can measure the production of carbon dioxide gas. By doing so, you can determine when the addition of more sugar does not increase the production of gas. This occurs when there is too much sugar for all of the yeast to metabolize in the two hours it takes to perform this experiment.

Objective
Learn about the role of yeast in nature and grow a form of yeast known as brewer's yeast in the presence of various amounts of sugar in order to measure the volume of carbon dioxide produced during sugar metabolism. Use this information to determine the best ratio of sugar to yeast for ideal sugar metabolism.

Materials

- 4 plastic bottles, 16-ounce (450-milliliter) size
- 1 plastic bottle, 32-ounce (1-liter) size
- Soap
- Water
- Label tape
- Marker
- Warm tap water, 98°F (37°C)
- 1 packet of brewer's yeast
- Measuring cup
- 6 tablespoons granulated sugar
- 4 balloons
- 4 binder clips
- Large bucket
- 6 quarts (6 liters) water
- Graph paper

Clean the four small plastic bottles and one large bottle with soap and warm water. Rinse the bottles thoroughly. Label the small plastic bottles "1," "2," "3," and "control," using label tape and a marker. Fill the large bottle almost to the top with warm water that is about 98°F (37°C). Once the water is in the bottle, the bottle should feel warm to the touch but not hot. Add one packet of yeast to the warm water and mix well by swirling it in a circular motion. Wait 5 minutes for the yeast to dissolve. You will know that the yeast have dissolved when the water becomes milky white. Using a measuring cup, pour 6 ounces (200 milliliters) of the yeast-filled water into each of the small bottles. Each of the four small plastic bottles should be about one-third full. Add 1 tablespoon of sugar to the first bottle, 2 tablespoons to the second bottle, and 3 tablespoons to the third bottle. Do not add any sugar to the fourth bottle so that you can use it as a control. Mix each of the solutions for 2 minutes by gently swirling the bottles. This will ensure that the sugar dissolves.

One at a time, stretch four balloons by blowing into them until they are full of air. Stretching the balloons will make it easier for the carbon dioxide gas generated by the yeast to fill them. Keep the balloons full for 2 minutes by twisting the end of the balloons and then holding them closed using binder clips. Release the air slowly.

Grasp the opening of a balloon and fit it over the top of the control bottle *(see figure 4.1).*

Repeat with the other bottles. Wait 2 hours. The balloons should begin to fill with carbon dioxide gas as the yeast start metabolizing (breaking down) the sugar.

Did you notice any difference in the size of the balloons after 2 hours? Which one was the largest? Which one was the smallest? If you do not see a difference after 2 hours, wait 2 more hours before you continue. Tie off each balloon while trapping the air inside.

Determine the volume of the gas in each of the balloons by a method known as displacement. Displacement works by submerging an object (such as a carbon dioxide-filled balloon) in a known volume of water contained in a bucket. You can determine the amount of gas by measuring how much water the balloon displaces. To do so, fill a large bucket with 6 quarts (6 liters) of water (you can use the 1 liter bottle to do this). Each time you fill the bucket with 1 quart (1 liter) of water, mark the upper level of the water on the side of the bucket using a marker. Remove 3 quarts (3 liters) of water from the bucket so that when you submerge the balloons you can measure the increase in volume using the measurement markings you just created.

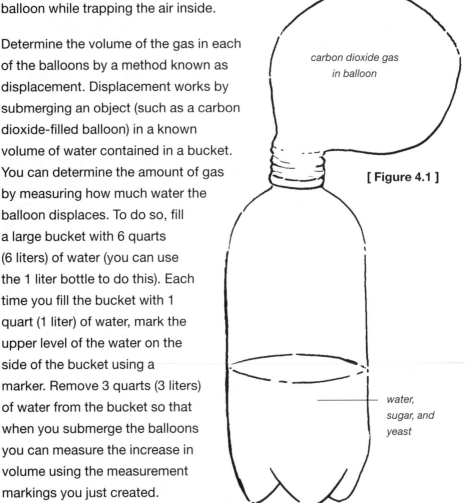

carbon dioxide gas
in balloon

[Figure 4.1]

water,
sugar, and
yeast

Measure the volume of water that the balloon displaces in the bucket after you submerge the balloon. Note the level of the water in the bucket. One balloon at a time, hold the balloon by the knot where you tied it and submerge it so that the entire balloon is below the surface of the water. Estimate the change in volume to the nearest $\frac{1}{4}$ liter or quart, then write it on the graph paper next to the name of the bottle you removed the balloon from. Repeat with the other balloons.

Next, make a graph of volume displaced by the balloon (on the vertical y-axis) versus tablespoons of sugar added (on the horizontal x-axis) on a sheet of graph paper *(see figure 4.2).*

Draw a dot on the graph for each balloon that you measured according to the volume of water displaced and the number of tablespoons of sugar that was in the bottle that that particular balloon was removed from.

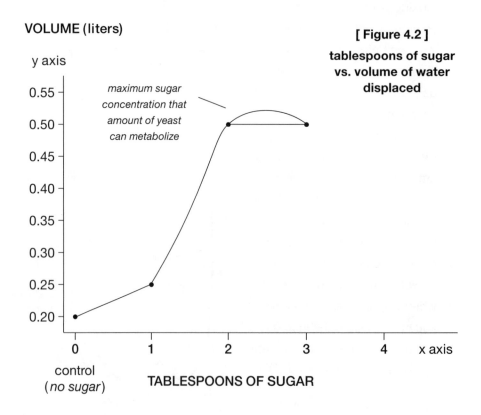

VOLUME (liters)

[Figure 4.2]

**tablespoons of sugar
vs. volume of water
displaced**

TABLESPOONS OF SUGAR

Connect the dots on the graph so that they form a line. You should notice a curve. The point where the curve levels off is the maximum amount of sugar that the quantity of yeast you used is able to metabolize into carbon dioxide gas over the period of time allowed in this experiment. It is at this point that adding more sugar will not result in greater gas production because the yeast will have metabolized all of the sugar they could over the given period of time.

Alternatively, you could determine how long it takes the yeast to consume all of the sugar in the bottle by waiting until the balloons stop expanding entirely. However, if the balloon inflates to the size of a softball, tie off the balloon and immediately add another balloon to the bottle and continue to measure the carbon dioxide released. Determine how long it takes the yeast to consume one, two, and three tablespoons of sugar.

Results

Which bottle produced the most gas? Why do you think this is so? Were 3 tablespoons of sugar too much for the yeast to metabolize during the period of time tested?

Variations

Determine if yeast can metabolize other food products using the same experimental setup as above. Your body is able to digest protein, fat, sugar, starch, and other carbohydrates and metabolize them for energy and growth. Determine if yeast can metabolize these items by adding 1 ounce (30 milliliters) of corn oil (fat) into one bottle with 6 ounces (200 milliliters) of yeast-filled water as above. Repeat with the same amount of something high in carbohydrates such as pancake mix. Using a fork, cut up 1 ounce (30 grams) of meat for the protein source. If you do not have a scale to measure the meat, just use your best estimate. Use the balloon method above

> ▶ *Yeast are used in the production of a wide variety of commercially used products such as bread and alcohol. Beer, wine, and several kinds of hard liquors are produced during a process known as alcoholic fermentation by the yeast* Saccharomyces cerevisiae. *This yeast is able to use a wide variety of food sources such as rice, wheat, barley, and rye. Plus, it produces the desired end product—alcohol—to which it has a very high tolerance. Other yeasts serve a much different role. For example, the yeast* Candida albicans *and* Cryptococcus *species are commonly found on our skin and mucous membranes (in our throat and mouth, for example), where they may help prevent infection. However, the very same yeast are known as opportunistic pathogens because when our immune system (red and white blood cells in our blood that fight off infections) are weakened, such as during a bout of the flu, opportunistic pathogens can attack us when we are most vulnerable to them.*

to compare the yeast's ability to metabolize each item. It may take the yeast longer to metabolize some of the food products, so wait at least 2 hours. Which foods were they able to metabolize (which balloons filled up after 2 hours)?

Bread Mold

Mold is a relatively simple type of fungus in terms of its appearance. Mold grows especially well in the dark and on damp surfaces that contain a lot of sugar or starch. Mold can be found naturally in a variety of places such as in soil, on fruits, and even under your kitchen sink. Bread mold is caused by a common fungus known as *Rhizopus stolonifer* by scientists. Growing mold is often as easy as leaving a piece of stale bread out on your counter for a few days.

Objective

Learn about mold contamination and determine if there are mold spores in your house by using bread. Determine if washing orange peels or treating them with Lysol is more effective at reducing the amount of mold that will grow on them.

Materials

- 2 types of bread (such as white and wheat, preferably store made)
- Plastic wrap
- 3 oranges
- 3 paper plates
- Marker
- Soap
- Lysol disinfectant spray
- 2 plastic cups, 8.5-ounce (250-millliter) size
- Soil
- Water

* *Adult supervision recommended*

When performing this experiment, be sure to take the following precautions. Wash your hands after touching the mold and dispose of it as soon as you are finished with the experiment. Never spray Lysol disinfectant on any type of food intended for consumption. Never eat anything that has been treated with Lysol.

Moisten a piece of bread and loosely wrap it in plastic wrap to keep it moist. Do not completely seal the plastic wrap. Repeat this with a different type of bread. Save the list of ingredients from the bread. Set the bread in a damp, dark place, such as under a bathroom sink. Take three oranges and set them each onto their own paper plate. Label the paper plates "washed," "unwashed," and "Lysol."

Wash one of the oranges with soap and water then return it to the plate labeled "washed." Spray a second orange with Lysol. Allow it to air dry for 5 minutes, and then place it back onto the plate labeled "Lysol."

Peel the oranges in the following order so that you do not cross-contaminate them with spores or chemicals. Peel the washed orange first, leaving the peels on the paper plate, and discard the orange. Peel the unwashed orange next, place the peels on the appropriately labeled paper plate, and discard the orange again. Last, peel the orange you sprayed with Lysol and place the peels on the appropriately labeled plate. Place all three plates of peels alongside the bread under the sink.

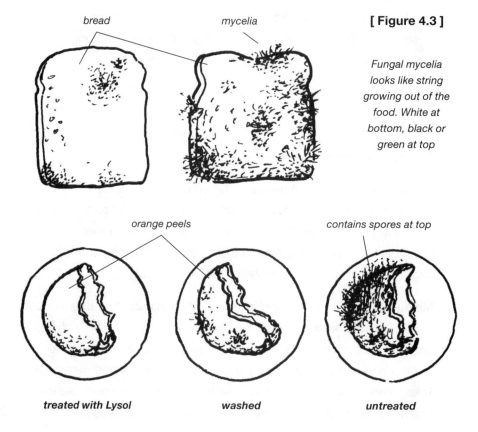

bread   mycelia

[Figure 4.3]

Fungal mycelia looks like string growing out of the food. White at bottom, black or green at top

orange peels   contains spores at top

treated with Lysol   **washed**   **untreated**

After 2 days, check the bread to see whether anything has begun to grow. If you do not see anything, wait another 2 days. You should notice a fuzzy carpet of green or black mold, which is a fungus, growing on the bread. This may be caused by the fungus *Rhizopus stolonifer*, commonly known as bread mold, or a variety of other molds such as *Aspergillus* or *Penicillium* species. Check the orange peels. You may notice a fuzzy green or white cottony film growing on them; this may be due to yeast or other fungi *(see figure 4.3).*

Did you notice a difference between the two varieties of bread? Some types of bread are more susceptible to mold than others. This is, in part, due to the presence of preservatives. Look at the list of ingredients from the bread and try to notice if anything in the ingredients such as a preservative may have led to the difference. Molds are commonly found growing on foods that contain a lot of sugar or starch (like jelly and potatoes) if they are left out at room temperature for a few days. Can you think of any other foods that are high in sugar or starch? Look at the ingredients in some of your favorite foods.

▶ *Mold and other fungi are common inhabitants of our environment. Fungi cause the majority of plant diseases; however, even humans are susceptible to some fungal diseases. Some human diseases caused by fungi include blastomycosis, cryptococcosis, histoplasmosis, and coccidioidomycosis. Plant diseases include root rot, leak (which affects strawberries), and downy mildew, which affects grapes. In 1885, Alexis Millardet, professor of botany at the University of Bordeaux, saved the vineyards of France from downy mildew by developing Bordeaux mixture, the first known fungicide.*

Results

Did you find bread mold in your house? If so, would you recommend storing unwrapped food where you found the mold? Did you notice a difference between the orange peels that were washed, unwashed, and treated with Lysol? If so, was washing them or using Lysol more effective at reducing mold?

Mushroom Spores

Many fungi are known for the mushrooms that they produce because they often appear very unusual and distinct. Shelf fungi grow on the sides of trees and look like a small shelf growing out of the side of the tree trunk. Mushrooms can grow to be quite large, and they often come in unusual shapes, colors, and sizes. Mushrooms can be thought of as tiny spore factories. They are great at releasing spores into the wild. One mushroom is capable of producing a large number of spores. In this next experiment, you can estimate how many spores one mushroom can produce.

Objective

Compare the total number of spores on a large versus a small mushroom fresh from the grocery store. Collect spores from a small and large mushroom for future use.

Materials

- 2 mushrooms from the grocery store (1 large and 1 small)
- Measuring cup
- Marker

- ▶ 2 pieces of white paper
- ▶ Plastic wrap
- ▶ 2 plastic sandwich bags
- ▶ 4 plastic cups, 3.4-ounce (100-milliliter) size
- ▶ Eyedropper
- ▶ Glass slides (or use plastic wrap as a substitute)
- ▶ Tweezers
- ▶ Microscope

Due to the small volumes of liquid used in this experiment, use the metric system for measurement. Because many mushrooms found in the wild are poisonous and even fatal, never eat a wild mushroom. They may make you very sick.

Allow the mushrooms from the grocery store to dry overnight at room temperature. This will make it easier for you to remove the spores. The mushrooms must be purchased within 24 hours of this experiment. The mushroom should feel dry to the touch the next morning.

Remove the stems by snapping them off with your fingertips *(see figure 4.4)*.

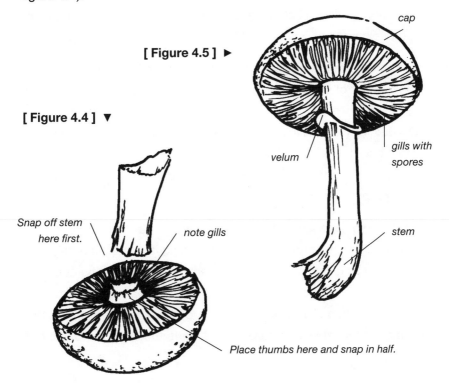

[Figure 4.5] ▶

[Figure 4.4] ▼

cap

velum

gills with spores

Snap off stem here first.

note gills

stem

Place thumbs here and snap in half.

On the underside of most, but not all mushrooms, is a thin membrane called the *velum (see figure 4.5).* Gently remove it with a pair of tweezers by poking a hole in it and ripping it off. This will reveal the gills (also known as the lamellae), which contain the spores. The gills look like thin slips of folded paper.

Place each mushroom cap on a piece of white paper with the cap facing upward and the gills facing down. Add a few drops of water to the top of the mushroom cap to assist in the dispersal of the spores onto the paper. Cover the top of the mushrooms with a piece of plastic wrap to prevent the spores from traveling in the air. Wait one hour for some of the spores to fall off the mushrooms. Gently tap on the mushrooms to release a few more spores onto the piece of paper. Only a small percentage of the spores will come off; however, this is more than enough for future use. Notice the pattern of the spores that have fallen onto the paper. This is known as a spore print and it is sometimes used to study and identify mushrooms. Fold the pieces of paper in half, then in half again, being careful not to lose any spores. Place each piece of paper into a plastic bag for use in a future experiment.

How many spores do you think one mushroom contains? To estimate the number of spores in each mushroom, you will need to dilute the spores as follows. Using a measuring cup, fill two plastic cups with 3.4 ounces (100 milliliters) of water. Label one cup "small" and the other one "large." The third cup will serve as a control. Fill the fourth cup with 1 ounce (30 milliliters) of water to serve as a rinse for the eyedropper.

Split the small mushroom in half by placing your thumbs on the center of the mushroom cap, then breaking it in two. Carefully remove a single gill with a pair of tweezers. Place it in the cup labeled "small." Using the eyedropper, mix the water in an up and down motion by alternately filling the eyedropper with water from inside the cup and then releasing the water back into the cup. Do not stir the water in the cup. Rinse the eyedropper in a clean cup of water. Repeat this process with the large mushroom, placing the gill in the cup labeled "large."

Add 1 drop of water from the control cup onto a glass slide or a piece of plastic wrap. Set it away from the mushrooms so that you will not carry over any spores onto the control slide. Count the total number of spores on your glass slide or piece of plastic wrap to get the number of spores per drop of water using a microscope at your school.

Determine the number of spores per 1 milliliter of water as in the example below. Multiply the number of spores on the slide by 10 because one drop of water from an eyedropper is approximately equal to one-tenth of a milliliter. Multiply the resulting number by the dilution factor, which is the volume of water you used to put the gill into. Use 100 since you used 100 milliliters. Multiply this number by the total number of gills, which is determined as follows. For each mushroom, using a pair of tweezers, count each gill, then press it down and out of the way in order to determine the total number of gills in each mushroom. Remember to add the gill that you removed to your total.

Determine the number of spores per mushroom according to the example below.

(For example, if you counted 200 gills and 100 spores on the slide, the number of spores per mushroom would be {(100 spores/slide x 10 drops/milliliter = spores/milliliter) x a dilution factor of 100} x 200 gills/mushroom = 2,000,000 spores per mushroom.

The final number in this equation is the number of spores per mushroom, which you can use to compare different mushrooms.

Results

There should be between 100 and 200 gills per mushroom. How many gills did you find on each mushroom? Do larger mushrooms have more spores than smaller mushrooms?

> ▶ *Some mushrooms can release 40 million spores in just one hour when they are actively releasing spores. Over a two-day period, some mushrooms can produce 18 billion spores (this is an 18 followed by nine zeros!). In some greenhouses, scientists have measured as many as 1 million spores per cubic meter of air. Can you imagine what it must be like to be allergic to mold spores?*

Growing Fungi

You can grow fungi on a special form of growth medium called *potato medium*. Fungi grow extremely well in the presence of starch, which is found in potatoes. Alternatively, you can add starch to the recipe for making growth medium, which you made in the experiment "Growing Bacteria."

Objective

Determine if soaking mushroom spores before growing them increases their ability to grow on potato medium. Also determine what dilution, if any, is best to grow them from.

Materials for the Potato Growth Medium

- ▶ Hand soap and running water
- ▶ 1 large baking potato, uncooked
- ▶ Potato peeler
- ▶ Plastic knife
- ▶ Water pot
- ▶ Oven mitts
- ▶ Fork
- ▶ Large spoon
- ▶ 1 box of Jell-O, any flavor
- ▶ 5 disposable plastic cups, 8.5-ounce (250-milliliter) size
- ▶ Plastic wrap
- ▶ 4 rubber bands

Materials for the Experiment

- ▶ Water, sanitized by boiling and allowed to cool while covered
- ▶ Mushroom spores *(see page 84)*
- ▶ Marker
- ▶ Tweezers
- ▶ Rubbing alcohol
- ▶ 4 disposable bathroom cups, 3.4-ounce (100-milliliter) size
- ▶ Notebook

✳ *Adult supervision recommended*

Preparing the Potato Growth Medium

Wash and peel the potato, then slice it into several small pieces using the plastic knife. Place the sliced potato into a large pot containing 2 quarts (2 liters) of water. Notice the level of the water just after adding the potato. Under adult supervision, place the pot containing the room-temperature water and the potato onto a stove. Bring the water to a boil. Allow the potato to boil in the water for 1 hour without a lid. At least once every 5 minutes, check the pot to make sure the water does not boil over. Check the water level and add warm tap water, as needed, back into the pot to maintain the same water level because the water will evaporate rapidly. Turn off the stove and wait 15 minutes for the water to cool. Wearing a pair of oven mitts, carefully pour off the extra water from the pot containing the potato slices. Once the pot has cooled to room temperature, carefully mash the potato slices in the pot, using a fork. Wash all of the cups and utensils with soap and warm water to remove any microorganisms that may be present.

Under adult supervision, prepare the Jell-O according to the instructions on the label with the following exception: replace $\frac{1}{2}$ cup of cold water with $\frac{1}{2}$ cup of potatoes.

After adding all of the ingredients, over the next 15 minutes mix the solution once every 2 minutes with a large spoon so that the solutions cools but remains well mixed. Fill each of the larger disposable cups with $\frac{1}{2}$ cup of this mixture.

Immediately after pouring the medium into the cups, cover each cup with plastic wrap. Place a rubber band around the plastic wrap to hold it in place. Refrigerate the cups for at least 3 hours to allow them to solidify.

Performing the Experiment

Dispose of any extra growth medium once you are finished with the experiment. If you still have some spores left over from the "Mushroom Spores" experiment, use them here. If not, collect some spores from a fresh mushroom (one that is no more than 1 day old) as instructed in the experiment on page 84.

Label five small cups "0 control," "1 oz control," "1 oz," "2 oz," and "3 oz" (or "0 control," "30 mL control," "30 mL," "60 mL," and "90 mL") *(see figure 4.6)*. These will serve as two controls and three different dilutions of your spores. Fill the cups with the appropriate amount of sanitized water. Remove the mushroom from the paper, then carefully fold the paper in half.

Sterilize the tweezers by soaking them in a solution of rubbing alcohol for 2 minutes. Remove the tweezers from the alcohol, allow them to air dry for 15 seconds, and then continue. The alcohol will kill any bacteria that may be on the end of the tweezers. Using the tweezers, scrape equal amounts of spores into the cups labeled "1 oz," "2 oz," and "3 oz" (just enough so that you can see them on the surface of the water) and to the cup labeled "0 control." Do not add any spores to the water in the 1 ounce control (30 mL control) cup. Allow the spores to rehydrate by soaking them for 2 hours.

Spread about 0.5 ounce (15 milliliters) of the spore-filled water from each cup onto the appropriately labeled cup of medium. The gelatin, which is porous, will absorb the water. Quickly replace the plastic wrap and rubber band onto the cups. The plastic wrap ensures that no bacteria or other fungi are introduced and grown on the medium. Repeat this procedure with the water from the 1 ounce control cup

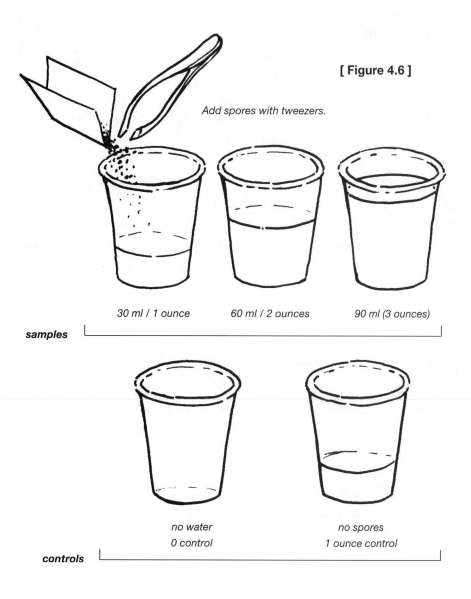

[Figure 4.6]

Add spores with tweezers.

30 ml / 1 ounce   60 ml / 2 ounces   90 ml (3 ounces)

samples

no water
0 control

no spores
1 ounce control

controls

(without any spores). Then add about half of the spores from the cup labeled 0 control (no water) to the appropriately labeled cup of medium.

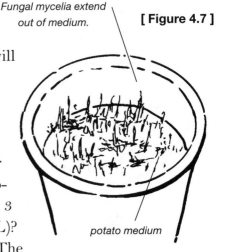

Fungal mycelia extend out of medium.

[Figure 4.7]

potato medium

Results

Within two to three days, mycelia will begin to form. If visible, they look like tiny strands of yarn, carpet, or string standing out of the medium *(see figure 4.7).*

Do you see mycelia on your potato medium? Which dilutions produced the most mycelia, 0, 1, 2, or 3 ounce (0 control, 30, 60, or 90 mL)? Record your results in a notebook. The dilution that worked the best is the one that has a lot of mycelia on it but is not completely covered with mycelia. You should not see any mycelia on the control (no spores) medium unless you accidentally contaminated it.

> ▶ *Mushrooms often sprout out of the ground together in a nearly perfect ring only to disappear within a week or two. This ring is known as a "fairy ring" because it was once believed that they magically formed where fairies danced. The ring is actually due to an undisturbed, out-ward growth of fungal hyphae from the original, central location. The grass is often greener in the center of this ring due to bacterial action on the older, decomposing hyphae in the center, which releases nutrients back into the soil and makes it available to the grass.*

Cloning

You can grow fungi by a method called cloning. *Cloning* is when you make an identical copy of an organism from a piece of its tissue or its cells. Fungi reproduce asexually, which is a form of cloning. However, in this experiment, you are going to grow fungi from a piece of its own tissue. This method can truly be called cloning.

Objective

Learn how to clone a mushroom from a piece of its own tissue, then determine what part of the mushroom is best to clone from.

Materials

- ▶ Soap and running water
- ▶ 1 fresh mushroom from the grocery store (purchased within 24 hours and kept refrigerated)
- ▶ Plastic knife
- ▶ Paper towels

- ▶ Rubbing alcohol
- ▶ 2 disposable cups with prepared potato growth medium *(see page 88)*
- ▶ Plastic wrap
- ▶ Rubber bands

＊ *Adult supervision recommended*

Wash your hands and the mushroom with warm tap water and a mild soap. Dry your hands and the mushroom using the paper towels. Using a plastic knife previously soaked in alcohol for sanitization, cut off a small piece of interior tissue from the cap and the stem of the mushroom. Place each of the slices of the mushroom onto a separate cup of potato medium. Cover the cups with plastic wrap and secure them with rubber bands. Let the mushrooms stand in a warm, dark place for 2 days.

Results

You should notice mycelia growing out of the mushroom slices directly onto the medium. They will appear grayish-white in color. If you do not see anything, wait another 2 days. Compare your results with what you saw in the previous experiment. Which part of the mushroom was best to clone from, the stem or the cap?

> ► *In 1997, researchers at the Roslin Laboratories near Edinburgh, Scotland, stunned the world by cloning the first sheep from adult sheep cells. While their intent is purely scientific, many people are worried about the implications this kind of technology may have, such as the eventual cloning of human beings for organs and other products. However, tightening guidelines and restricted government funding will likely prevent that from occurring any time soon.*

5

Last but Not Least: The Protozoans

(Kingdom Protoctista)

The last kingdom is called Protoctista (formerly Protista). Currently, the members of this group include the protozoans, slime molds, algae, diatoms, and other organisms that do not fit neatly in the other four kingdoms. However, many scientists would argue that this is not a natural group of organisms and would like to see it abandoned, while many botanists would prefer to place the algae and slime molds in the kingdom Plantae.

Many, but certainly not all, of the organisms in this group are single-celled creatures that can be found floating or propelling themselves by means of flagella in freshwater, saltwater, or moist soil. Some are even found in fish tanks and swimming pools. Other members of this group, such as the brown and red algae, are multicellular, quite large, and have complex life cycles. They are found mostly in the oceans.

The unicellular organisms of this kingdom are usually referred to as *protozoans*. However, if you are referring to the multicellular organisms as well, they should be referred to as *protoctists*. Many protozoans have characteristics in common with plants, animals, and fungi. For example, euglena, amoebas, and water molds obtain their nutrition by photosynthesis, ingestion, and absorption, respectively. Euglena are found mostly in freshwater where they use chlorophylls *a* and *b* to convert solar energy into chemical or food energy. Amoeba are found in almost every freshwater body. They resemble animals in that they obtain food by ingestion. They are best known for the way they glide through the water by means of pseudopodia, as seen under a microscope. *Pseudopodia* are fingerlike projections that form in amoeba due to the movement of the cell contents. Other protoctists include the red and brown algae, which make up seaweed and are most commonly found in tropical and other marine environments.

Growing Protozoans

When you think of all the living things in a lake or pond, fish, snails, worms, and even crayfish may come to mind. While this is true, there are a great number of other creatures that can be found living in a lake or pond that you may not notice without further investigations. In fact, most of the organisms living in a pond are tiny microscopic organisms that you cannot even see with the unaided eye. Many of these creatures are called protozoans.

In nature, you can find many different types of protozoans. They are most common in freshwater, saltwater, and moist soil. They can be found throughout the year, but they are higher in number during the summer months.

Objective

Capture protozoans from two different regions of pond sediment to estimate and compare their numbers and general cell types and characteristics.

Materials

- Sink
- 5 clear plastic bottles, 16-ounce (500-milliliter) size
- Measuring cup
- 1¼ cups (315 milliliters) water, sanitized by boiling and allowed to cool
- Grass clippings (preferably still green)
- 4 cups water
- Notebook
- 2 sources of pond sediment (see below for details)
- Lamp
- Marker
- Label tape
- Microscope slides
- Cover slips for slides
- Microscope
- Eyedropper

In a sink, rinse out five clear plastic bottles with running tap water. Fill two plastic bottles with ½ cup of sediment from the upper 1 inch (2.5 centimeters) of sediment from a nearby pond (or large mud puddle if no pond is available) because protozoans thrive in these types of environments. Fill a third plastic bottle with ½ cup of sediment that is from at least 2 inches (5 centimeters) below the surface of the sediment from the edge of a pond or puddle. The fourth bottle will serve as a control to determine if the grass clippings already have protozoans growing on them, which could add to the number you would find in the bottles by the end of the first week *(see the next experiment on page 101).*

Add $\frac{1}{4}$ cup of the sanitized water to each of the four bottles. Add $\frac{1}{4}$ cup of water to the fifth bottle, which will serve as a rinse for your eyedropper later in the experiment. Using the marker and some label tape, label the bottles "shallow soil plus grass," "shallow soil, no grass," "deep soil, no grass" and "control plus grass."

Viewing Protozoans

Using a marker and label tape, label four microscope slides as above. Gently mix each solution containing the protozoans you wish to observe under a microscope (all four bottles in this experiment) by swirling each one individually for 5 minutes. Fill up an eyedropper with the water from one of the bottles *(see figure 5.1).*

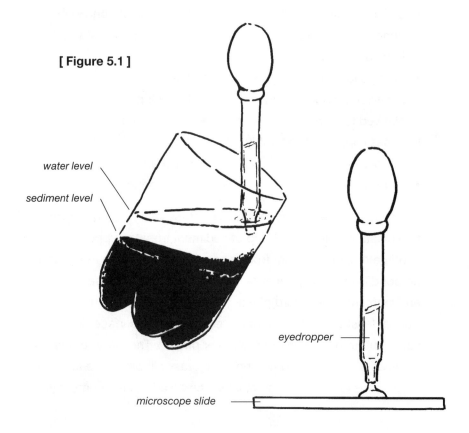

[Figure 5.1]

water level

sediment level

eyedropper

microscope slide

Place one drop of the water from each bottle onto the appropriately labeled microscope slide. Make sure to rinse the eyedropper with water between each use.

Place a cover slip over each drop of water and then view the water under the microscope under low magnification. Move the focus knob until the field of view becomes clear. Look for protozoans at 100x magnification. At this magnification, you will not be able to see bacteria without a special dye, but you will be able to see protozoans, which will appear like tiny cells moving around in the water *(see figure 5.2).*

Look for different types of protozoans such as *motile* (capable of movement), nonmotile, and green cells in each of the four slides. Many protozoans can be seen as oval cells moving in a corkscrew fashion through the water. Most protozoans have flagella during some part of their life cycle. *Flagella* are whiplike extensions of the cell, which serve to propel the cells. Others protozoans, such as diatoms, often resemble diamonds with long spikes protruding from their surface. Some, but not all, will appear green due to the

[Figure 5.2]

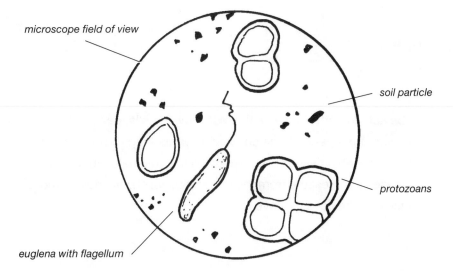

microscope field of view

soil particle

protozoans

euglena with flagellum

presence of chlorophyll. Others may appear brown or yellow-brown due to the presence of other pigments.

Write down a description of each different type of cell you see in your laboratory notebook. Make a note of how many of each type you see. If you notice any differences, make a note of it. You should not see any cells on the "control plus grass" microscope slide containing a drop of water from the "control plus grass" bottle (because you did not add the grass yet). However, try it just in case—this will serve as another control.

BOTTLE	NUMBER OF CELLS	SIZE, SHAPE, COLOR, AND APPEARANCE OF CELLS	WATER/SOIL ADDED (CUPS)
Control plus grass—before grass added			
Shallow soil plus grass			.25/.5
Shallow soil, no grass			.25/.5
Deep soil, no grass			.25/.5

To be able to better observe the fast-moving cells, remove some of the water from beneath the cover slip by touching the corner of the cover slip with a tissue. This decreases the volume of liquid and increases the pressure from the cover slip, which will make it more difficult for the cells to move.

Add 1 ounce (30 grams) of crushed-up grass to the bottle labeled "plus grass." Add the grass to the control bottle so that you can determine if the increase in protozoans is due to succession, which you will learn about in the next activity, or if there were protozoans on the grass. The grass will serve as a source of food for some of the organisms. Place the bottles in a sunny and warm place, such as under a lamp.

Results

You should not see any cells on the control microscope slide because there should not be any protozoans in boiled tap water. However, you should see several cells from water from pond sediment. Did you notice as many cells in the deep soil sample? There is less oxygen and fewer nutrients in deeper soil; therefore, you will likely see fewer cells in it. However, some sediment may have gotten mixed around, so don't be surprised if you get different results. As you get better at sampling soil from these types of environments, your results may vary slightly.

▶ *Diatoms include a variety of unicellular marine and freshwater algae (protozoans) that form deposits often on the floor of oceans, rivers, and streams. Dried-up crusts of diatoms are used in reflective paint on highways, license plates, and street signs. They are also used as abrasives in metal polishes and some toothpaste.*

Protozoan Succession

A mixed population of protozoans in pond sediment often changes over time, especially when the sediment is disturbed or modified in some way. In some instances, this process is known as *succession*. Succession occurs in plants and animals communities, too. Succession is the progressive, and often predictable, changing of the organisms in a community over time. In plants and animals, this might occur after a forest fire, erosion, flood, or other natural disaster. It also occurs on a smaller scale, as you will see in the protozoans. You can determine if this phenomenon occurs in a protozoan community as a result of the addition of a food source.

Objective

Determine if the composition of protozoans in a sample of sediment from a pond changes over the course of 1 week due to the addition of a food source such as grass clippings.

Materials

- ▶ Shallow sediment samples with and without grass from previous experiment *(see page 96)*
- ▶ Control plus grass sample from previous experiment
- ▶ Cover slips for slides
- ▶ Microscope
- ▶ Measuring cup
- ▶ 1 ounce (30 grams) granulatedsugar
- ▶ 1 cup (250 milliliters) water
- ▶ Marker
- ▶ Label tape
- ▶ Microscope slides
- ▶ Cover slips for slides
- ▶ Eyedropper

After allowing the protozoans from the previous experiment to grow and multiply for 1 week, count the number of cells in one drop of liquid from each bottle to determine if the number or type of protozoans in the bottles has changes over time.

Viewing Protozoans

Using a marker and label tape, label four microscope slides as "shallow soil plus grass," "shallow soil, no grass," and "control plus grass." Gently mix each solution containing the protozoans you wish to observe under a microscope by swirling all four bottles in this experiment individually for 5 minutes. Fill up an eyedropper with the water from one of the bottles. Place 1 drop of the water from each bottle onto the appropriately labeled microscope slide. Make sure to rinse the eyedropper with water after each use.

Place a cover slip over each drop of water, then view the water under the microscope under low magnification. Move the focus knob until the field of view becomes clear. Then look for protozoans at 100x magnification. At this magnification, you will not be able to see bacteria (without special dye) but you can see protozoans, which will appear like tiny cells moving around in the water *(see figure 5.2)*.

Look for different types of protozoans such as motile, nonmotile, and green cells on each of the four slides. Pay special attention to any differences from the first day of this experiment *(see previous experiment, page 96)*. Write down a description in your laboratory notebook of each type of cell you see. Make a note of how many of each type you see, and if you notice any differences, make a note of that too. Even after 1 week, you should not see any cells on the control microscope slide containing a drop of water from the control bottle. Write down your observations in your laboratory notebook.

If the cells are moving too quickly, you can slow them down using a mixture of 50 percent sugar and 50 percent water. You can make this solution by adding 1 ounce (30 gram) of granulated sugar to a plastic bottle containing 1 ounce (30 milliliters) of water. Replace the cap and mix the sugar-water mixture by swirling it for several minutes, allowing the sugar to dissolve completely. Once the solution becomes clear, the sugar has dissolved. Place 2 drops of pond water into 1 drop of sugar water on a microscope slide. This should help to slow down the ciliated protozoans, making it easier to count them. After 1 week, did you count more protozoans in the jar to which you added the grass?

Results

Did you find any protozoans in the control jar at the end of 1 week? If so, they were likely already on the grass; therefore, you should subtract the number of cells you counted in 1 drop of control water from the number you counted in 1 drop of water from the bottle labeled grass because they were due to the grass, not changes due to succession *(see formula below)*.

Did you notice succession, or a change in the types or number of cells that you saw over the course of a week due to the addition of the food source? How do you think succession might affect larger animals during catastrophic events, such as deforestation (removal of trees from a forest) or a forest fire? Determine how many protozoans there are in 1 quart (1 liter) of pond water according to the example and formula below.

SAMPLE	CELLS AT START/END
Shallow soil plus grass	8/16
Shallow soil, no grass	8/8
Control plus grass	0/0

In this example, there was an increase of 8 cells per drop of culture here: $(8 - 8 - 0 = 0) + (16 - 8 - 0 = 8) = 8$. Assume there are about 11,300 drops per quart (10,000 drops per liter). How many protozoans would there be in 1 quart (1 liter) of this water?

Variations

Repeat the above experiment using a sample of soil from your backyard instead of sediment from a pond. Add an equal volume of soil from your backyard to two clean jars. Add an equal volume of the water that was previously boiled to each jar. Add 1 ounce (30 grams) of grass clippings to each jar. Mix the solution for 10 minutes. Tilt the jars to the side, then remove a sample of the water using an eyedropper. Determine the number of protozoans in 1 drop of the water at the beginning, and end of 1 week to look for succession.

> ▶ *Cellulose is a common plant material that mammals such as ourselves are unable to digest because we lack an enzyme called* cellulase. *Mammals such as moose, deer, antelope, cows, and goats have a structure known as a* rumen *in their digestive tract where cellulose is digested. These animals are called ruminants because they have a rumen, which is the section of the stomach where crude digestion takes place. Ruminants themselves do not produce the enzyme cellulase; however, they do possess protozoan and other microorganisms in their rumen that do.*

Conclusion

THIS BOOK STARTED OUT by asking you the question "What is biology?" Can you define biology now? In a way, this is a trick question. No one person can give you an exact definition of what biology is because it means many things to different people. However, after experimenting with members of the five kingdoms of life you should be able to formulate your own definition. More important, you should understand that biology is the study of a diverse group of organisms, some large, some small, some common, and some unique, and all manage to survive in a world filled with other creatures with their own unique habits and habitats.

This book used the scientific method to study the five kingdoms; that is, it took you from observation to hypothesis formation, to experimentation, and finally to interpreting your results. The best part about biology is that it can be anything you want it to be. Once you understand the scientific method, you can use it to study biology or any other science in an informed, logical, and educated way.

Now that you've experimented with organisms from each kingdom you will probably begin to notice more of the biology that surrounds you in everyday life. Biology is the science of life. It is everywhere and you cannot live without it or in the absence of it. Having completed the experiments in this book, you may begin to notice how living things interact with one another and how plants and animals are interdependent. One thing is for sure: biology is often unpredictable and strange, but it always follows scientific principles that you can observe and interpret, and if you're very lucky, no one in the world has ever realized them before.

Resources

Table of Conversions

The following is a list of conversions that you will need throughout this book. These may come in handy elsewhere as well.

Length

1 inch = 2.5 centimeters

10 millimeters = 1 centimeter

1 meter = 1.09 yard

1 centimeter = .393 inch

Weight and Volume

1 gallon = 4 quarts = 8 pints = 3.79 liter

1 quart = 32 fluid ounces = 0.946 liter

1 liter = 1 kilogram

1 gallon is approximately equal to 8.8 pounds

1 kilogram = 1000 grams = 2.20 pounds

1 pound = 16 ounces = .454 kilograms = 454 grams

1 ounce = 28.4 grams

Temperature

32°F = 0°C

212°F = 100°C

75°F = 25°C

Books

The following is a list of science experiment books that beginning biologists may also enjoy.

Anderson, Margaret Jean. *Bizarre Insects.* Springfield, NJ: Enslow Publishers Inc., 1996.

Appelhof, Mary. *Worms Eat My Garbage: How to Set Up and Maintain a Worm Composting System.* Kalamazoo, MI: Flowerfield Press, 1997.

Conklin, Gladys Plemon. *The Bug Club Book: A Handbook for Young Bug Collectors.* New York: Holiday House, 1966.

Leahy, Christopher. *Peterson First Guide to Insects of North America.* New York: Houghton Mifflin Company, 1987.

Mandell, Muriel. *Simple Kitchen Experiments: Learning Science with Everyday Foods.* New York: Sterling Publishing Co., 1993.

Stamens, P., and J. S. Chilton. *The Mushroom Cultivator.* Olympia, WA: Agarikon Press, 1983.

Suzuki, David. *Looking at Insects.* New York: John Wiley & Sons, 1992.

Web Sites

The following Web sites will assist you in finding out more about plants, animals, and other biology-related information. You can check your experiment results against what you find on these Web sites.

www.garden.com
A great resource for gardening questions. Links for purchasing supplies as well as other resources.

www.niehs.nih.gov/kids
From the National Institute of Health, this site has tons of exercises for teachers and students in the area of science and biology.

www.little-scientists.com
Little Scientist is a Web site for children containing fun and exciting projects for the classroom and home with a list of links to other sites.

www.eskimo.com/~billb/edu.html
This is a huge list of links to dozens of science-related sites.

www.spartechsoftware.com/reeko
This Web site contains a lot of science experiments for children of all ages.

www.swiftnaturecamp.com
Swift Nature Camp is located in Illinois and is a great way to vacation and learn about biology.

www.awesomelibrary.org
A list of educational resources online. Rated one of the best.

www.biology.arizona.edu
The biology project is an online science experiment site that saves you money because you do not have to use supplies or reagents, just your computer, to experiment with science.

www.peterpauls.com
Peter Paul's Nursery is a great source of unique plants such as the Venus's-flytrap and other carnivorous plants, as well as plant supplies.

californiacarnivores.com
Another place to purchase carnivorous plants at a great price. Fast delivery options and retailer of gardening and other carnivorous plants equipment.

www.gardenweb.com
The Garden Web is a fabulous resource about plants. You will find the answer to almost any gardening question here.

www.geocities.com/CapeCanaveral/5229/n_grvtro.htm
Information about gravitropism including before and after images.

www.insectlore.com
Order insect kits online for the experiments in this book or experiments of your own at this site.

www.wormdigest.org
All about worms. Seemingly every question about worms is answered here.

www.oldgrowth.org/compost/wormfaq.html
More frequently asked questions about worms and composting.

www.uga.edu/protozoa/protocol.htm
Are you interested in protozoans? If so, this is the Web site for you.

www.factsonfile.com
This is a publisher of science and other experiment books commonly found in schools and libraries nationwide.

www.ex.ac.uk/bugclub/bugid.html
This interactive Web site lets you determine what species an insect belongs to. Simply answer the questions about your specimen online until you figure out the species.

www.pbs.org/wgbh/nova/teachersguide/odyssey/
    odyssey_sp3.html
This site describes an alternate means of creating a worm bin.

www.allthingsorganic.com
Kits for composting, decomposition, and worm bins.

www.skyport.com/brownvillemills/ssp.html
Purchase all types of supplies such as yeast, sugar, and other powders and have them sent right to your home for experimentation.

www.healthsavers.com/hsd_home.html
Creams, lotions, and antibiotic ointments for experimenting at a great discount.

www.accessexcellence.org
This is a Web site for students interested in biology with a great deal of resources, links, and online projects.

www.ent.iastate.edu/list/k-12_educator_resources.html
Lesson plans for grades K–12 mainly in the area of entomology.

Supply Sources

You can order supplies from these companies if you cannot find what you need near your home.

A great place to buy worms, if you cannot purchase them locally:

> *Appropriate Technology Transfer for Rural Areas (ATTRA)*
> P.O. Box 3657
> Fayetteville, AZ 72702
> Phone: (800) 346-9140

A wide variety of Fungi spores and supplies:

> *Fungi Perfecti*
> P.O. Box 7634
> Olympia, WA 98507
> Phone: (360) 426-9292
> Fax: (360) 426-9377

> *American Type Culture Collection*
> 10801 University Boulevard
> Manassas, VA 20110-2209
> Phone: (703) 365-2700

A great store for yeast and baking supplies:

> *Brownville Mills*
> P.O. Box 145
> Brownville, NE 68321
> Phone: (800) 305-7990

The best stores to buy carnivorous plants by mail, phone, or over the Internet:

> *Peter Paul's Nurseries*
> 4665 Chapin Road
> Canandaigua, NY 14424-8713
> Phone: (716) 394-7397
> Fax: (716) 394-4122
> E-mail: info@peterpauls.com

> *California Carnivores*
> 7020 Trenton-Healdsburg Road
> Forestville, CA 95436
> Phone: (707) 838-1630
> Fax: (707) 838-9899
> E-mail: califcarn@aol.com

> *Greenscapes*
> White Deer Court
> Huntington, NY
> Phone: (631) 421-4422
> Web site: http://members.aol.com/gscapeine

Information about raising carnivorous plants, free seeds, and a great place to visit them in the wild:

> *North Carolina Botanical Garden*
> University of North Carolina at Chapel Hill
> C.B. 3375, Totten Center
> Chapel Hill, NC 27599

Phone: (919) 962-0522
Fax: (919) 962-3531

If you need plastics, pH, iodine test paper, or other gadgets, try these places:

Beer and Wine Hobby
180 New Boston Streets
Woburn, MA 01801-6206
Phone: (800) 523-5423
E-mail: shop@beer-wine.com

Red Bank Brewing Supply
111 Oakland Street
Red Bank, NJ 07701
Phone: (732) 842-7507

The best place for insects, butterflies, and moth collections:

Carolina Biological Supply Company
2700 York Road
Burlington, NC 27215
Phone: (800) 334-5551

Glossary

Agar A gelling agent prepared from seaweed.

Antibacterial hand soaps Soaps that contain a chemical such as an antibiotic that kills or inhibits the growth of microorganisms.

Anticoagulants Compounds that prevent the blood from clotting normally after a cut or abrasion.

Aseptic technique A method of handling supplies and equipment so that they remain free of unwanted microorganisms.

Bacteria Single-celled microscopic organisms. Most absorb nutrients from their surrounding environment.

Cells The basic unit of structure in all living things. Cells make up tissue, and groups of tissue make organs.

Chitin A nitrogen-containing polysaccharide found in some animals such as insects and in most fungi.

Chlorophyll A pigment in plants used to convert solar energy into chemical or food energy.

Chloroplasts The cellular organelles containing pigments and enzymes and are the site of photosynthesis in plants.

Circulatory system A network that nutrients such as oxygen and proteins and waste travel through to and from all parts of the body in most animals.

Decomposition The breaking down of complex substances into simpler ones.

Elements The basic unit of chemicals. For example, water is made up of two atoms of hydrogen and one atom of oxygen.

Embryos Reproductive structures that eventually result in a new offspring under the appropriate conditions. Plant embryos are very different from animal embryos.

Fungi Complex organisms that absorb nutrients from their environment. They are more complex than bacteria.

Gravitropism A response by plants that results in growth toward (positive gravitropism) or away from (negative gravitropism) gravity.

Growth medium A nutrient-containing liquid or solid substance used to grow microorganisms such as bacteria.

Hemoglobin An iron-containing pigment in the blood of humans and other animals that delivers oxygen to tissue.

Hypocotyls The portion of the germinating seed between the radicle (future root) and cotyledons (temporary leaves).

Hypothesis An assumption made to test its observed consequences.

Melanin A brown-colored pigment found in skin that protects it from the harmful effects of UV rays, which have been shown to cause skin cancer.

Metabolism The collection of chemical reactions that take place within cells. It is the process by which organic compounds are either broken down or put together in living organisms.

Microbiology The study of microscopic life. *Micro* means small.

Micronutrients Chemical compounds such as iron that are required in very small quantities in our diet.

Mitochondria Energy-producing bodies within the cells of plants and animals.

Mold spores Structures used by a variety of fungi for asexual reproduction. Many people are allergic to them.

Multicellular organisms Creatures that are made up of many cells, such as animals. Plants, most fungi, and animals are all multicellular. Bacteria and some fungi are not.

Nucleus The dense structure in most cells that contains the genetic material in all organisms except bacteria and cyanobacteria.

Organelles Structures inside of cells, such as the nucleus, chloroplasts, and mitochondria in eukaryotic organisms, that allow division of labor within cells.

Photosynthesis The process by which plants convert solar energy into chemical or food energy using sunlight.

Polysaccharides Compounds made up of many sugar molecules.

Prokaryotes Organisms such as bacteria that do not contain a nucleus or other membrane-bound organelles such as chloroplasts or mitochondria.

Pseudopodia Fingerlike projections that form in amoebas by the movement of the cell contents that assist in locating food and motility.

Respiration The exchange of carbon dioxide, a waste product of our cells, with oxygen, which is required by all of the cells in our body.

Saprophytes Organisms that live on dead or dying organisms for food.

Scientific Method A systematic procedure for obtaining information in a logical and reproducible manner. In order it consists of observation, hypothesis formation, experimentation, and explanation or interpretation.

Seed-bearing plants Plants that contain a specialized reproductive structure known as a seed.

Seeds Reproductive structures in plants that form when a female egg is fertilized by a male pollen grain.

Species Groups of organisms that are capable of breeding and whose offspring are also capable of breeding.

Standing crop The mass of living plant material that can be found in a given area at a given point in time.

Starch A complex insoluble carbohydrate. It is the main storage molecule of plants.

Stomata Tiny openings on the surface of leaves in plants where gas exchange occurs. Stomata also open and close in response to environmental conditions such as temperature and humidity.

Transpiration The loss of water by plants at the surface of structures such as leaves through tiny openings called stoma, where gas exchange occurs.

Unicellular organisms Organisms comprised of a single cell, such as many bacteria, yeast, and protozoans.

Vermiculite A porous rocklike substance.

Viruses Microscopic organisms that require a living host to live. They cannot grow on their own.

Bibliography

Alexopoulos, C. J., and C. W. Mims. *Introductory Mycology*. 3rd ed. New York: Wiley, 1979.

Allen, Jessie and Marc Greene. *More Science Experiments on File*. New York: Facts on File, Inc., 1991.

Anderson, R. O., and M. Druger. *Exploring the World Using Protozoa*. Arlington, VA: National Science Teachers Association Press, 1997.

Baily, Jill. *Animal Life: Form and Function in the Animal Kingdom*. New York: Oxford University Press, 1994.

Bold, H., Alexopoulos, C. J., and T. Delevoryas. *Morphology of Plants and Fungi*. 5th ed. New York: Harper Collins Publishers, 1987.

D'Amato, Peter. *The Savage Garden*. Berkeley, CA: Ten Speed Press, 1998.

Graf, Albert Byrd. *Exotic House Plants Illustrated*. East Rutherford, NJ: Roehrs, 1973.

Grim, W. C. *Recognizing Flowering Wild Plants*. Harrisburg, PA: Stackpole Books, 1968.

Hickman, F. M., and C. P. Hickman, Jr. *Laboratory Studies in Integrated Zoology.* St. Louis: Times Mirror/Mosby College Publishing, 1988.

Hine, Robert. *The Facts on File Dictionary of Biology.* 3rd ed. New York: Checkmark Books, 1999.

Margulis, L., J. O. Corliss, M. Melkonian, and D. J. Chapman, eds. *Handbook of Protoctista.* Boston: Jones & Bartlett Publishers, 1990.

Margulis, L., and K. V. Schwartz. *Five Kingdoms: An Illustrated Guide to the Phyla of Life on Earth.* 2nd ed. New York: W. H. Freeman and Company, 1988.

Patent, Dorothy Hinshaw. *How Insects Communicate.* New York: Holiday House, 1975.

Tortora, G. F., B. R. Case, and C. L. Case. *Microbiology: An Introduction.* Redwood City, CA: Benjamin Cummings, 1992.

Index

RAJ